The NHL Lockout Baby Boom

Hockey Humor and Other Absurdities

J. Alexander Poulton

OVER TIME BOOKS

© 2013 by OverTime Books
First printed in 2013 10 9 8 7 6 5 4 3 2 1
Printed in Canada

All rights reserved. No part of this work covered by the copyrights hereon may be reproduced or used in any form or by any means—graphic, electronic or mechanical—without the prior written permission of the publisher, except for reviewers, who may quote brief passages. Any request for photocopying, recording, taping or storage on information retrieval systems of any part of this work shall be directed in writing to the publisher.

The Publisher: OverTime Books is an imprint of Éditions de la Montagne Verte

Library and Archives Canada Cataloguing in Publication

Poulton, J. Alexander (Jay Alexander), 1977–
    The NHL lockout baby boom : hockey humor and other absurdities / J. Alexander Poulton.

Includes bibliographical references.
ISBN 978-1-897277-77-5

    1. Strikes and lockouts—Hockey—Humor. 2. National Hockey League—Humor. I. Title.
GV847.4.P69 2013   331.892′81796962640207   C2013-901510-8

Project Director: Deanna Howell
Editor: Wendy Pirk
Cover Image: Joy Dirto

We acknowledge the financial support of the Government of Canada through the Canada Book Fund (CBF) for our publishing activities.

Canadian   Patrimoine
Heritage   canadien

PC: 1

CONTENTS

Introduction 4

CHAPTER 1:
Lockout Defined 7

CHAPTER 2:
A Season Without Hockey 16

CHAPTER 3:
The Owners, the League and Mr. Bettman 31

CHAPTER 4:
Hockey Fan Revolution 64

CHAPTER 5:
Our Favourite Teams 92

CHAPTER 6:
To Err is Hockey Player 109

CHAPTER 7:
Back to Hockey!!! 140

CHAPTER 8:
Fun with Hockey 166

CHAPTER 9:
More Fun with Hockey 195

CHAPTER 10:
Diary of a Locked-out NHLer 225

Notes on Sources 231

INTRODUCTION

Let's face facts. Any professional sport lockout is no laughing matter. It is not just the livelihood of the players and the owners at stake—many people are involved with and depend on professional sports to pay their rent. Concession staff, security guards, servers at local restaurants, sports merchandise stores…the list goes on. However, in among the lost dollars and sad fans, there is much humor to be found, because when you are facing the third NHL lockout in less than 20 years, you need to laugh or you will start crying.

During the 2012–13 NHL lockout, the constant bickering between the players, owners and the evil Count Bettman made fans a little stir-crazy, and the plethora of YouTube videos and hilarious tweets that spewed forth during the 119 days of the lockout gave me an idea. Why not turn all this negativity and boring talk of hockey-related revenue (another way of saying "your money") into something we can all laugh at, because after the latest lockout, hockey fans need something to laugh about. So I began to scour the sports pages and Internet for jokes and stories surrounding the lockout, and I came up with this book.

In these pages you will find funny stories about how some of the players spent their lockout days, including Philadelphia Flyers goaltender Ilya Bryzgalov's Russian space camp adventure or how fans from the 2004–05 lockout got so fed up with Bettman and the league that they sued for control

INTRODUCTION 5

of the Stanley Cup. Speaking of Bettman—boy people don't like him, so naturally there are a million jokes and stories to tell. I selected the ones with the least amount of swearing and violence. Bettman, though, sometimes gets a lot of unfair criticism because he is the voice of the owners, so naturally I take them to task and subject them to a few barbs of cheeky humor.

Luckily, though, the 2012–13 lockout did not result in an entirely canceled season, or Canadians surely would have gone into withdrawal and become totally unpredictable, like the rioting mob of Vancouver Canucks fans. Most fans were able to cope, reluctantly of course, in their own ways, but a small few rebelled against the evil empire. Steve Chase, an expat Montrealer living in Los Angeles, used his experience in the film industry to produce a short film called "Just Drop It" that basically asked fans to boycott the NHL. No games, no merchandise, nothing hockey related. Although it was a decent idea, asking Canadians to not pay attention to hockey is like asking a moth not to go toward the light. We have to—it's in our blood!

The lockout was good for a few people. Wives across the land could finally watch those wonderful Jennifer Aniston movies they always wanted to see. They would find their husbands sitting in front of blank TVs mindlessly flicking stations, looking for any hockey news or praying the sports networks would replay old games in full. But luckily the players and the owners got back to the negotiating table and worked out a deal. So, while the wives now lament the loss of date night, husbands everywhere have returned to the bars and basements to scream at the television and get angry with the players—for the right reasons.

Now that hockey has returned and relative peace has been brokered between the players and the owners for at least another eight years, take the time to crack open this book and have a laugh at the insanity that is the world of modern hockey—and the people that surround it, play it and love it.

CHAPTER 1

Lockout Defined

My plan, at first, was to draw a picture of a man scratching his head while looking at a picture of Gary Bettman and a group of players surrounded by numbers, because this would be an accurate portrait of how most people feel when trying to understand the third NHL lockout in almost 20 years, but my publisher told me that I had to be a little more descriptive. Fine!

Let's start with the very first labor-relations problem the National Hockey League faced, way, way back in 1957. Yup, 1957, when, after years of living under the oppression of NHL owners, the players decided to get together and form an association to protect their rights. The idea of forming a union started with Hall of Fame legend "Terrible Ted" Lindsay. In 1952, the Detroit

> Q: What is hockey?
>
> A: I don't know, I haven't seen anyone play hockey for years.

Red Wings forward was appointed to the board of the NHL's Pension Society, where he got a taste of the politics that run behind the scenes of the spectacle on the ice—and he did not like what he saw. He got a look into an NHL where owners were getting rich off sold-out arenas, television deals and merchandising while many players were forced to take summer jobs during the off-season to make ends meet. Lindsay's biggest problem was that, as a member of the Pension Society, he was not allowed to see the books to the players' pension fund, to which they contributed 20 percent of their average $5000 salary. Lindsay's frustration with the NHL owners would stew over the next few years until he came up with the idea of forming a players association to collectively take on the owners. He first approached Montreal Canadiens defenseman Doug Harvey, who had served with him on the NHL Pension Board. Harvey liked the idea, and by February 1957, the two men had signed up every player in the league to the fledgling association. Lindsay knew that the NHL bosses would not like his idea, but he was never one to back down from a fight.

The NHL bosses, however, well versed in business and squashing union sentiment, were quick to move on Lindsay and other principal players in the movement. Detroit Red Wings boss Jack Adams responded by removing Lindsay's captaincy and later trading him to the basement-dwelling Chicago Blackhawks. Adams further insulted Lindsay by making false statements about his salary to the press and even went as far as to hold up a fake contract to prove his lies. Many of the Red Wings players bought into Adams' lies and opted out of the new players association, effectively squashing Lindsay's hopes of a united front. As the Red Wings players began to opt out, so did many players on other teams, and the idea of a players union was shelved. The notion remained in the back of the players' minds, but it did not resurface until a wonderful man named Alan Eagleson arrived on

LOCKOUT DEFINED

scene and took the players' best interests to heart (in case you didn't catch it, that was sarcasm).

Alan Eagleson, a Toronto-based lawyer, started off his involvement with the NHL and its players with good intentions, but as the saying goes, absolute power corrupts absolutely. Eagleson, with the assistance of a few members of the Toronto Maple Leafs, strong-armed the NHL owners into accepting the existence of the NHL Players Association (NHLPA) in 1967. Bob Pulford was elected as the first president, and Eagleson was given the title of executive director. This era—which lasted until 1991, when it was discovered that Eagleson had been stealing money from the players for years— was relatively peaceful in terms of labor relations, and it also saw the average player salary jump from the low thousands to an average of around one million dollars.

Once the NHLPA got rid of Eagleson, the relationship between the association and the league started to dissolve. The first strike action came in 1992 with an NHLPA-initiated action. The players saw an opportunity as their collective bargaining agreement (CBA) was coming up for renewal at the end of the 1991–92 season. The league had grown by leaps and bounds over the years, and the players saw the amount of cash being generated and wanted to claim some for themselves. The 1992 strike lasted only 10 days before NHL president John Ziegler capitulated to many of the players' demands, including increased playoff bonuses, increased control over the licensing of their likeness and player-favorable changes to the free agent system. The resulting overwhelmingly lopsided contract infuriated the NHL owners, so they removed long-time president Ziegler from his job and replaced him with Gil Stein. The new president, though, was a mere placeholder as the NHL owners looked for a more business-suitable candidate who would take the owners' interests to heart, expand the league and get back some of the contract terms they had lost over the years.

In 1993, on the 75th anniversary of the league, the board of governors replaced Stein with the new NHL commissioner Gary Bettman. Although the former basketball commissioner expanded the business and took hockey into new markets, the relations between the players and the managers in the years since have been contentious, to say the least, and as they fight over millions of dollars, the fans have been the ones to suffer.

In his first year in office, Bettman began working to secure the position of all the owners of the league, and the first major hurdles he faced were how to deal with the small market teams, tying players' salaries to revenues and establishing a salary cap. The league-initiated lockout stretched from October 1, 1994 to January 11, 1995. Because the players and the league were unable to come to an agreement, the season was played without a collective bargaining agreement. While the hope was to solve the

Lockout motto: Today Is the First Day of the Rest of this Mess.

LOCKOUT DEFINED

problem of the small market teams in the league, the lockout did more harm than good and eventually forced the closure of the Winnipeg Jets, the Quebec Nordiques and the Hartford Whalers. The first lockout left a bitter taste in many fans' mouths for the new NHL business model and a rabid hatred for the man they perceived to be the cause of all the problems.

After the first lockout-interrupted season, the NHL seemed to progress through the 1990s and into the new millennium in relative peace. The league ended off the decade with the fond farewell tour of Wayne Gretzky and the expansion of the league into new markets, but beneath all those fuzzy feelings, a simmering resentment between the players and the league was reaching its boiling point. The league was also losing its fans. Goal production was down, there were the brief yet painful experiments with the glowing puck, the toe-in-the-crease rule (ask the 1999 Buffalo Sabres about that one), and a fan base in the U.S. that did not really give a damn about the more southern teams. The failures of the game, linked to the failure of the 1994–95 lockout to come to any significant agreements, basically set up another confrontation between the players and the league. This would result, in 2004–05, in the first complete lost season in the history of the league and just the second time that the Stanley Cup would not have a winner. (The first time was in 1919, when the Stanley Cup final between the Montreal Canadiens and the Seattle Metropolitans was canceled because of the Spanish influenza epidemic.)

During the 2004–05 lockout, Bettman again tried to convince the players association that the only way to have all the teams prosper was to link the players' salaries to the league revenues to achieve cost certainty. Bettman presented a list of ways to achieve this cost certainty, and the NHLPA completely rejected the offers, claiming that they were just a way of implementing a salary cap, which the players said they would never accept. The boardroom negotiations continued through the fall and winter until in January it was decided that both sides were too far apart and the season had to be canceled. In this lockout, the players took most of the blame for the loss of the season because of their refusal to take a salary cap (which they ended up accepting anyway, argh!) while the league and the owners looked rational and prudent when looking at the numbers.

The loss of the complete season was difficult for many people to stomach, especially Canadians, who had to drastically alter their winter season social lives and who no longer had the All-Star game, or the Winter Classic, or the trade deadline to look forward to and discuss with friends. Male friends would sit in bars and simply stare at each other. Sometimes they would talk about other sports, but it wasn't the same Canada, as the nation (and some parts of the U.S.) was locked into a deep darkness that saw the light only once a new contract was signed and the Sidney Crosby lottery kicked off a whole new fever.

When hockey returned, the fans and cash-hungry owners breathed a sigh of relief. To welcome fans back to the NHL, the league instated new rule changes to speed up the game and up the amount of goals scored. It was an immediate success as young stars like Crosby and Ovechkin became the new marketable faces of a league trying to put the latest lockout out of the minds of the fans. And it seemed to work. From 2005 onward, the league saw a remarkable increase in revenue and a new influx of fans more passionate about the game than ever.

But as the previous CBA was drawing to a close, another dark cloud began to loom over the NHL, and as the Los Angeles Kings raised the Stanley Cup over their heads at the end of the 2011–12 season, there was little talk of optimism for the coming season. The owners wanted their master of ceremonies to tackle a few prickly issues with the players. At issue for the owners were desires to reduce the players' guaranteed 57 percent share of hockey-related revenues, introduce term limits on contracts, eliminate salary arbitration and change free agency rules. The NHLPA, now led by Donald Fehr, was not happy with the demands, and as a result we got another bloody lockout.

And so, hockey fans everywhere were sent back into their dark place, but something different occurred this time around: the fans were no longer taking sides, and that was bad news for both parties.

Losing a half season and another full season was bad enough, but try to take away pro-hockey again and you risk the wrath of the hockey fan. Many of them took to the Internet to voice their opinions on the subject, making for some very humorous YouTube videos.

The players and the league did not want to tarnish the image of pro-hockey more than it already had been, so they sat down together at a table until they finished their vegetables and came out with a decent agreement everyone could be happy with. Once peace reigned again, hockey returned—after 119 days of lockout for another shortened season of 48 games. Fans tried to remain distant and cold, telling hockey they couldn't come back because they had a headache, but once the festivities began, fans accepted the NHL's roses and forgave them. In Canada at least, fans lined up in frigid temperatures in all cities (except Vancouver, where they lined up in the rain) to watch open and free practices and gushed over their favorite players like lovestruck teenagers. In the United States, the job has been a little harder. Owners knew that once the lockout was over they would have difficulty getting the fans to come back because the game just isn't the same cultural institution that it is in Canada. Teams like the Tampa Bay Lightning were selling tickets at ridiculously low prices, offering free food vouchers and basically begging the fans to return. Although the forgiveness has been steadily increasing, I want all parties to remember.

LOCKOUT DEFINED

WE THE FANS control the NHL. Do this again, and WE REVOLT!

Now that the boring stuff is out of the way, let's get to making fun of everyone and find out what shenanigans the pros and non-pros have been up to in hockey's absence.

≪ CHAPTER 2 ≫
A Season Without Hockey

With three lockouts in less than 20 years, having no hockey to watch has begun to affect society in a variety of ways—some predictable and some completely a surprise.

Consequences of the Lockout

- Dentists across North America were forced to close their business because of the lack of patients.

- Hat makers across North America also suffered. Without the hat trick, people kept the hats on their heads instead of throwing them on the ice.

- Without hockey, fathers across the country slowly emerged from their man caves to discover that their children had aged and that they had wives.

- When Gary Bettman announced the end of the lockout, millions of Americans said, "Lockout what?"

- When the lockout was announced, all traces of Don Cherry suddenly disappeared from the Earth, and when it came back, boom!, there he was again as if nothing had happened. No one knows what happens to Don Cherry when hockey is not being played. Some say he goes into hibernation, while others say he requires hockey to exist—kind of like Santa and Christmas cheer, except Cherry needs pucks and blood on the ice.

This is What Happens When There is No Hockey

A blonde wants to go ice fishing. She's seen many books on the subject, and finally, after getting all the necessary tools together, she makes for the nearest frozen lake. After positioning her comfy stool, she starts to make a circular cut in the ice.

Suddenly—from the sky—a voice booms, "THERE ARE NO FISH UNDER THE ICE!" Startled, the blonde moves farther down the ice, pours a Thermos of cappuccino and begins to cut another hole.

Again, from the heavens, the voice bellows, "THERE ARE NO FISH UNDER THE ICE!" The blonde, now quite worried, moves way down to the opposite end of the ice, sets up her stool and tries again to cut her hole. The voice comes once more, "THERE ARE NO FISH UNDER THE ICE!"

She stops, looks skyward and asks, "Is that you, Lord?"

The voice replies, "NO, THIS IS THE MANAGER OF THE HOCKEY RINK."

News Conference

At a news conference, a reporter asks one of the NHL owners, "Is your lack of movement on the CBA negotiations due to ignorance or apathy?"

The owner replies, "I don't know, and I don't care!"

The U.S. Women's Hockey team beat Canada to win its second consecutive World Hockey Championship title. In related news, without NHL hockey, it's a very, very slow day in the world of sports.

Time Off

With nothing to do during the lockout, goaltender Roberto Luongo goes into a bar near his Florida home, and the bartender tells him there is a standing offer for all patrons: free liquor to anyone who can pass a test. So Luongo asks what the test is.

"Well," the barkeep says, "First you drink an entire gallon of our home-brewed moonshine all at once, without stopping or throwing up. Second, we got a gator out back with a sore tooth, and somebody has to take it out. Third, we got a woman upstairs who has never had an orgasm, and you gotta go take care of her."

"Done," says Luongo arrogantly. "I can drink anything and still pull off miracles. You're on!"

So he grabs the moonshine, downs it in only a few gulps, then staggers outside, shrieking, "Here gator, gator, gator!"

The rest of the bar patrons hear roaring and thumping and the most god-awful hollering and thrashing about, then sudden silence. Luongo stumbles back into the bar, his shirt torn, bleeding from one eye and shouts, "Now where is that b*tch with the sore tooth?"

A SEASON WITHOUT HOCKEY   19

While he is sitting on the sun deck of the local golf club, Marvin is hit in the head with a ball. By the time the offending golfer chases down his shot, Marvin has an ice pack on his head and is ripping mad.

"I'm going to take you to court!" Marvin screams at the golfer. Upon noticing that the golfer is none other than the Canadiens' P.K. Subban, Marvin says, "I'll sue you for five million dollars!"

Distressed, Subban says meekly, "I said 'FORE!'"

With a triumphant look, Marvin announces, "I'll take it!"

Out on the Course Foul

Mike Cammalleri is out on the golf course during the lockout when he meets a woman on the first tee and agrees to join her for the round. To his surprise and disappointment, she turns out to be a good player and beats him by several strokes. Although he is angry about losing, he takes a shining to the woman and buys her a drink in the bar afterward. He then offers to drive her home. She is so grateful that halfway through the ride, she asks him to pull over and then gives him the best oral sex of his life.

> Did you hear about the change Canada Post made to their stamps? There used to be a picture of Gary Bettman on them, but people didn't know what side to spit on!

The following day, with the lockout still in progress, Cammalleri is back out on the course and bumps into her again. They agree to play another round. Much to his annoyance, she wins again by several strokes. This goes on for the rest of the week. By the following week, Cammalleri is really annoyed. He is, after all, a very competitive player and hates losing, but the oral sex is spectacular. So he arranges to take things further with the woman and gets a hotel room for the weekend. But when he tells her his plans, she bursts into tears.

"What's wrong?" he asks.

"I can't go with you," she sobs. "You see, I'm a transvestite."

He is furious. "You dirty, stinking cheater!" he rages. "You've been playing off the ladies tee all week!!!!"

Fighters Always Fight

Chris Neil walks into an Ottawa bar with his arm in a cast. "What happened to you? You're not even playing hockey," says the bartender.

"I got into a fight with Gary Bettman."

"Bettman? He's only a little guy! You could have taken him. He must have had a weapon or something. Please Chris, tell me you weren't beaten up by Gary Bettman," says the bartender.

"He had a shovel in his hand," says Neil.

"Didn't you have anything in your hands?"

"I did—his daughter. And a beautiful thing she is, but not much use in a fight."

A man has been stranded on a desert island for 10 years and in that time hasn't seen another living person. Then one day, to his amazement, a gorgeous blonde steps out of the sea wearing a wetsuit and scuba gear. He can hardly believe his eyes as she walks up to him and starts caressing his beard. "How long has it been since you last had a cigarette?" she asks.

"Ten years," he stutters.

She slowly and seductively unzips her wetsuit and pulls a pack of cigarettes and matches from between her cleavage. He gratefully accepts a cigarette, lights it and sighs. "Thank you so much. I've been dying for a smoke for years."

When he has finished the cigarette, she asks, "How long has it been since you last tasted whiskey?"

"Ten years."

She pulls a bottle of whiskey out of her scuba gear and hands it to him. He drinks almost half of it.

"Gee, this is amazing. Are you some sort of angel bringing me everything I want?" he asks.

"Maybe. Now, how long has it been since you last had some real fun?"

The man's face suddenly lights up. "Don't tell me! Hockey is finally back!"

Shane Doan's wife is getting irritated by how friendly he is being with the young girl across the street. It has been more than 100 days since the lockout started, and having him around the house all the time is wearing on her nerves. One day she looks out the window and sees Shane and the girl talking in her front yard. So, she picks up the phone and calls the girl. "Tell my husband to get his ass across the street!" she demands.

The girl replies sweetly, "Ma'am, that's where he's been getting his ass for weeks."

Too Much Time on Hand

Vincent Lecavalier has plenty of time to kill during the lockout, so he decides to go down to a lake near his home in Tampa, but when he gets there, he realizes he forgot his swimsuit. There seems to be no one around, so he decides to take a risk and jump in naked. An hour later, he climbs out and is just about to get dressed when he sees two old ladies approaching. He hastily grabs a small bucket that is lying on the ground, holds it over his privates and breathes a huge sigh of relief because the water was very cold. But when the old ladies stare at him, he starts to feel a little weird.

One of the ladies says to him, "You know, I have a special gift. I can read minds. And I bet I can read yours."

Lecavalier laughs. "You think you know what is going on in my mind?"

"Yes," she says. "Right now, I bet you are thinking that the bucket you're holding has a bottom."

Not all players are Sidney Crosby, making eight million dollars per year, so during the lockout a few players have to find extra work.

One player reports for his first day of work as a sales assistant at a major department store. The sales manager shows him around and is passing through the gardening department when he hears a customer asking for a packet of grass seed.

"Will you be needing a hose to water your new lawn?" interrupts the sales manager.

"Yes, I probably will," says the customer. "Thank you, I'll take a hose as well."

"And what about fertilizer," suggests the sales manager, "to make the grass grow green and strong?"

"Good idea," responds the customer.

"And of course there are always the troublesome weeds," continues the sales manager. "So you'll be wanting a bottle of weed killer to keep them down. The large bottles work out to be the most economical."

"Right," says the customer.

"And once your lawn is green and lush, how about a new mower to make it look perfect?"

"Why not," says the customer, who then pays for everything and leaves.

The sales manager takes the young hockey player/salesman aside and says, "See, that's how it's done. That customer came in for only one item but ended up leaving with five. That's good sales technique. That's what I want you to emulate."

The hockey player/sales assistant is then posted in the pharmaceutical department. A man comes in and asks for a pack of tampons.

The assistant seizes his chance. "Are you sure you wouldn't like to buy a lawn mower, as well?"

"Why would I want to do that?" the customer replies.

"Well, your weekend's ruined, so you might as well mow the lawn."

A Salesman in Dallas

A Canadian salesman is in Dallas, Texas, for the first time. He wanders into a bar and drinks a pretty fair number of straight vodkas. In a couple of hours, he is quite drunk.

Suddenly, he notices Gary Bettman on the news on the bar's big screen TV. "There is the biggest horse's ass who ever walked the face of this earth. There is no bigger horse's ass than Gary Bettman!"

With that, the cowboy sitting next to him stands up, punches him in the jaw and sits back down on his bar stool.

"Owwwww," says the salesman, picking himself up off the floor. "I better be careful what I say around here. I had no idea I was in Gary Bettman country."

"You ain't in Bettman country," says the cowboy. "Don't insult us. This here is HORSE country!"

Because of the lockout, some "lucky" Canadian small town doesn't get the honor of being named Kraft Hockeyville. Yeah, your town gets the corporate sponsorship of a company that makes Oscar Mayer wieners and fought against legislation that would force them to label if any genetically engineered food appears in their products. Yay!

Terrible News

First Russian: "Did you hear the terrible news? The Canadian hockey player who caused the Moscow Dynamo to lose the Gagarin Cup in the final, he died."

Second Russian: "Nyet! When did he die?"

First Russian: "Tomorrow!"

The receptionist at the NHL head offices answers the telephone after learning that Gary Bettman has just been fired.

"Is Gary Bettman there?" asks the person on the line.

"I am sorry sir, but Mr. Bettman was fired yesterday," the receptionist answers.

"Is Mr. Bettman there?" the person asks again.

The receptionist is a little confused and says, "Perhaps you did not hear me, but I am afraid that Mr. Bettman was fired yesterday."

"Is Mr. Bettman there?" asks the person one more time.

"Sir, do you understand the words that are coming out of my mouth?" she asks angrily. "Bettman was fired!"

"I understand you perfectly," the person says. "I just cannot hear it often enough."

Too Much Time Off

A wife insists that her husband accompany her to church every Sunday, now that he isn't watching hockey all the time because of the lockout. It is an ordeal for him, and he always has difficulty staying awake. She is aware of his predicament, so one week she takes along a hatpin to poke him with every time he falls asleep.

Five minutes into the service, just as the husband is dozing off, the preacher asks, "Who created the universe?"

The wife pokes her husband with the hatpin, and he yells loudly, "My God!"

A few minutes later, the husband's eyes are shutting again just as the preacher asks, "And who died on the cross for your sins?"

The wife jabs her husband's side with the hatpin, and he shouts, "Jesus Christ!"

Shortly afterward, the husband is asleep once more. The wife pokes him with the hatpin just as the preacher asks, "And what did Eve say to Adam the second time she was pregnant?"

The husband wakes with a start, jumps to his feet and yells, "By God, if you poke me with that thing one more time, I'm gonna break it off."

A man and his wife walk into a dentist's office. The man says to the dentist, "Doc, I'm in one hell of a hurry! I have two buddies sitting out in my car waiting for us to go play hockey. So forget about the anesthetic and just pull the tooth and be done with it. We have a 10:00 AM faceoff at the best rink in town and it's 9:30 already. I don't have time to wait for the anesthetic to work!"

The dentist thinks to himself, *My goodness, this is surely a very brave man asking to have his tooth pulled without using anything to kill the pain.* So he asks the man, "Which tooth is it, sir?"

The man turns to his wife and says, "Open your mouth, honey, and show him."

No Winter Classic? Fine!

Even with the return of the NHL in January 2013, the league was forced to cancel a few of its high-profile events, including the All-Star game (Sorry, Columbus, it would have been the first time you got to witness a real hockey game) and the Winter Classic, which was supposed to feature the Detroit Red Wings versus the Toronto Maple Leafs.

The Winter Classic has become a yearly NHL staple after the success of the first outdoor NHL game in 2003 between the Edmonton Oilers and the Montreal Canadiens. The game usually occurs over the New Year's holiday and features a weekend of special events including an oldtimers game followed by the actual outdoor league game between the two teams. It has become an incredibly popular showcase for the NHL and a unique way of reaching new fans who would never have given the sport a chance—a gimmick, but an effective one.

When it was announced that the Detroit Red Wings would be playing the Toronto Maple Leafs at Michigan Stadium in Ann Arbor, there was a lot of hype surrounding the game because since the Canadiens and Oilers played in the 2003 Heritage Classic, no other Canadian team had played in the outdoor game. (Which is strange given that Canada is so bloody cold in the winter and that the Boston

Bruins and the Philadelphia Flyers in 2010 played in the rain—kinda made it lame.) So getting the Maple Leafs and the Red Wings out for a game under the stars was to be the NHL's most anticipated outdoor game.

> **Q:** *What does NHL stand for?*
> **A:** *No Hockey Losers.*

However, as the 2012 lockout progressed into the 60th and 70th days, it looked as if the fate of the 2012–13 Winter Classic was sealed. To no one's surprise, the game was eventually canceled and Michigan Stadium was to be left empty, with nary a sports fan cheering or being happy. Well, fear not, sports fans. No, the NHL did not re-schedule, but someone else stepped in to fill the void. The Harlem Globetrotters would not be the team most people would pick to fill in for hockey but, ever the creative sportsmen, the Globetrotters took the NHL's loss and turned it into their opportunity.

On January 7, while the NHL owners and the players were locked in a boardroom complaining about revenue percentages, the Harlem Globetrotters laced their shoes and took on the Global Select (formerly the Washington Generals) at the Ice Rink at Millennium Park in Portage, Michigan. Yes, that's right, I said ICE.

"We hope the NHL can return to the ice as quickly as possible," said Globetrotters CEO Kurt Schneider. "But in the meantime, we thought the Globetrotters could help fill the void of professional sporting events on an ice surface. And it's only fitting we play this outdoor game in Michigan, as our tour continues in Kalamazoo the next day."

Basketball on ice! That's crazy! It is, but it's the Harlem Globetrotters; it's not like the games count for something. So strapping some fancy custom spikes to their Air Jordans, the towering athletes hit the ice to play a game of basketball. The Globetrotters had a little help in preparing to play on the strange b-ball court when Detroit Red Wings alumnus Kevin Miller joined the Trotters to help them get a feel for playing sports on ice. Playing basketball in unconventional places is, however, the bread and butter of the Globetrotters and they have played on beaches (how does the ball bounce?), in empty swimming pools and even at the Vatican (holy b-ball). The people of Michigan were much appreciative of the Globetrotters taking the place of the Wings and the Leafs, and a few thousand people came out to watch them beat the Select (surprise!). Entertaining, yes—but it still wasn't hockey.

CHAPTER 3
The Owners, the League and Mr. Bettman

When it was announced that another lockout would soon take hockey away from North America, this time around it was the owners and especially the diminutive NHL commissioner Gary Bettman that received the most flak from the media and the fans—and one can see why. You had owners and the league collectively making billions of dollars and they were arguing over percentage points with the players. It smacked of the worst kind of greed. So what did people do? Well, they lashed out, and poor old Bettman became the target of much of the derision. So this chapter was rather easy to put together because that little man is not very well liked.

News Flash: This just in! Gary Bettman has been locked out of his car. He has entered into negotiations with the automobile, but talks have broken down and no further meetings have been scheduled.

Guidelines for Owners

When in charge, ponder.

When in trouble, delegate.

When in doubt, mumble.

How to Feel Better after an NHL/NHLPA Meeting

Just sit back, relax and feel the tension leave your body...picture yourself near a stream. Birds are chirping in the crisp, cool mountain air. Butterflies flutter in the breeze. Leaves rustle. Nothing can bother you here. Nobody knows this secret place. You are in complete seclusion. The soothing sound of a gentle waterfall fills the air with a cascade of serenity. The water is clear. You can easily make out the face of the person whose head you are holding under the water.

There now...don't you feel better?

> **Q:** What do you call five NHL owners standing in a row?
> **A:** A wind tunnel.

A man dies and is taken to his place of eternal torment by the devil.

As he passes sulfurous pits and shrieking sinners, he sees a man he recognizes as Gary Bettman snuggling up to a beautiful woman.

"That's unfair!" he cries. "I have to roast for all eternity, and Gary Bettman gets to spend it with a beautiful woman."

"Shut up," barks the devil, jabbing the man with his pitchfork. "Who are you to question that woman's punishment?"

What Makes Gary Bettman Special

- When *you* take a long time, you're slow.
- When Gary Bettman takes a long time, he's thorough.
- When *you* don't do something, you're lazy.
- When Gary Bettman doesn't do something, he's too busy.
- When *you* make a mistake, you're an idiot.
- When Gary Bettman makes a mistake, he's only human.
- When *you* do something without being told, you're overstepping your authority.
- When Gary Bettman does the same thing, he's showing initiative.
- When *you* take a stand, you're being bull-headed.
- When Gary Bettman does it, he's being firm.
- When *you* overlook a rule of etiquette, you're being rude.
- When Gary Bettman skips a few rules, he's being original.

Top 10 New NHL Slogans

10. It's Like An Episode of *Cops* On Ice!

9. See For Yourself What Canadian Blood Looks Like.

8. The "H" Is For "Hematoma."

7. It's Like Watching Really, Really Primitive Dentistry.

6. A Sport That Combines Your Two Favorite Things—Ice Skating and Head Trauma.

5. You Can't Spell "Unhealthy" Without "NHL."

4. Share the Excitement, or We'll Beat Your Brains In With a Piece of Wood.

3. We Will Play Hockey When We Feel Like It!

2. Don't Worry, Kids—They're Just Saying "Puck."

1. He Shoots, He Scars.

The NHL is that ex that calls you drunk at 3:00 AM. You know it's wrong to answer. They hurt you, and you said you'd never get back together, but man is the hockey really, really, really good.

You're Fired!

Poor Brian Burke—the Leafs don't play a single game and he gets fired for being a bad general manager.

At the Table

Gary Bettman complains during an NHL staff meeting that people don't respect him enough. Trying to change the attitude in the office, he comes in the next day with a sign for his door that reads I AM THE BOSS.

One of the employees, apparently not appreciating the change, sticks a note on the sign. It reads, YOUR WIFE WANTS HER SIGN BACK.

New Idea

One afternoon, two women are sitting at a bar discussing their love lives. One woman looks at the other and says, "You know, 80 percent of all men think that the best way to end an argument is to make love."

"Well," says the other woman, "that would certainly revolutionize the game of hockey!"

Hockey is like politics. You've got the left wing, the right wing and the center, and they're always beating the hell out of each other! And occasionally both sides don't show up and argue for months over money, and nothing gets done.

> Owner logic: "We're overpaying him, but he's worth it."

NHL Boss Morality Tale

The body has been created, and all the parts want to be boss.

The brain says, "I should be boss because I control the whole body's responses and functions."

The feet say, "We should be the boss because we carry the brain about and get him to where he wants to go."

The hands say, "We should be the boss because we do all the work and earn all the money."

And so it goes on and on, with the heart, the lungs, and the eyes, until finally the *sshole speaks up. All the parts laugh at the idea of the *sshole being the boss. So the *sshole goes on strike, blocks itself up and refuses to work.

Within a short time the eyes become crossed, the hands clench, the feet twitch, the heart and lungs began to panic and the brain becomes feverish. Eventually they all decide that the asshole should be the boss, so the motion is passed. All the other parts do all the work, while the boss just sat and passed out the sh*t!

Moral of the story: You don't need brains to be a boss—any *sshole will do.

I just rear-ended Gary Bettman with my car. He gets out and says, "I am not happy." So I say, "Well then, which dwarf are you?"

Canadian Hockey Temperature Conversion Table

50°F (10°C)
- New Yorkers try to turn on the heat.
- Canadians plant gardens.

40°F (4.4°C)
- Californians shiver uncontrollably.
- Canadians sunbathe.

35°F (1.6°C)
- Italian cars won't start.
- Canadians drive with the windows down.

32°F (0°C)
- Distilled water freezes.
- Canadian water gets thicker.

0°F (–17.9°C)
- New York City landlords finally turn on the heat.
- Canadians have the last cookout of the season.

–40°F (–40°C)
- Hollywood disintegrates.
- Canadians rent some videos.

–60°F (–51°C)
- Mount St. Helens freezes.
- Canadian Girl Guides sell cookies door-to-door.

−100°F (−73°C)
- Santa Claus abandons the North Pole.
- Canadians pull down their ear flaps.

−173°F (−114°C)
- Ethyl alcohol freezes.
- Canadians get frustrated when they can't thaw the keg.

−460°F (−273°C)
- Absolute zero; all atomic motion stops.
- Canadians start saying, "Cold, eh?"

−500°F (−295°C)
- Hell freezes over.
- Hockey fans put up with ANOTHER LOCKOUT!

News Flash: This just in! Citing rising costs, Gary Bettman locks his wife out of the house. Saying that he could no longer afford to keep his wife in the lifestyle that she is used to, NHL commissioner Gary Bettman takes a drastic step and locks his wife, Audrey, out of their suburban mansion.

"It's a tough decision for me to make, but given the proportion of my annual income and the revenue sharing that my wife requires, the financial situation has reached an unacceptable level. Having failed to come to an agreement on revenue sharing and other issues, I am forced to lock her out of the house until we can come to a sustainable agreement," says Bettman to a throng of reporters outside his home.

"We had been very fortunate over the last few years, but with the recent downturn in the economy and the fact that my job as NHL boss is on the line after a third NHL lockout under my watch, I cannot justify keeping my wife's lifestyle up to the previous years' standards. Frankly, I'm left with no option," says Bettman. "But I am hopeful that my wife and I can come to some sort of mutual agreement that will benefit the Bettman household and ensure its future prosperity."

Mrs. Bettman says of the lockout, "This is just a tactic by Gary. I am privy to the finances of our household, and it is a money grab on his part. I believe it is for his increased golfing budget. I will not stand for this, and I will be having regular meetings with Gary to get this resolved."

Though the Bettmans are confident of a resolution, Mrs. Bettman told this reporter privately that a similar situation occurred in the past, and they were forced to call in a professional mediator to get it resolved. In the meantime, Mrs. Bettman has been seen with a Russian billionaire looking very happy.

Bettman in Retirement

After retiring as commissioner of the NHL, Gary Bettman has just one remaining wish in life—to meet the Pope in person and confess his many sins to the man closest to God. He is willing to stay in Rome for as long as it takes to achieve his ambition. Week after week, he joins the crowds in Saint Peter's Square but never gets any closer than the occasional glimpse of His Holiness on the balcony. As Bettman is bemoaning his lack of success to an English tourist, the tourist offers to sell him his ticket for a garden party that the Pope is hosting in the Vatican the next day. Bettman willingly pays $1000 for the ticket. He notices that the invitation stipulates full morning dress, so he hurries off to an exclusive Italian tailor.

The next day Bettman goes to the Vatican dressed in his morning suit and top hat and stands in a line of guests waiting for the Pope to appear. The guests are drawn up in two lines facing each other so that the Pope can walk down one line, turn and then go back along the other line. When the Pope finally appears, there is polite applause. Bettman waits expectantly as the Pope proceeds down the first line, but to the dismay of everyone in the room, he speaks to nobody. Instead, he merely waves vaguely as he passes Bettman and makes his way down the line.

> The 2012–13 lockout is now officially known as the Gary Bettman Hat Trick.

A homeless person, looking hopelessly out of place in his tattered and smelly clothes, occupies the last position in the line. But, to everyone's surprise, the Pope stops when he reaches the tramp, puts his hands on the poor man's shoulders and whispers something in his ear.

Bettman thinks quickly. It is clear that the Pope will only talk to a hobo, someone who is in need of comfort, so Bettman grabs hold of the homeless man and persuades him to trade clothes. Dressed in tattered rags, Bettman rushes to the end of the second line and waits for the Pope to reach him.

Once again the Pope speaks to no one until he reaches the bum-like figure at the end of the line. Bettman can hardly contain his excitement as the Pope stops and looks at him. Then the Pope puts his hands on Bettman's shoulders and whispers in his ear, "I thought I told you a moment ago to get the hell out of here!"

Riding

During a break from lockout talks, Gary Bettman goes on vacation and has a terrible experience riding a horse. For no apparent reason, the beast becomes wild and angry, completely out of control. Bettman tries desperately to hang onto the reins, but the horse is so unpredictable that he is eventually thrown off. As he falls, his foot gets caught in the stirrup and his head bounces repeatedly on the ground as the horse refuses to stop or even slow down. Finally Bettman is saved when the mall security guard unplugs the machine.

Deal

An NHL lawyer is approached by the devil with a proposition. The devil says he'll arrange for the lawyer to win every negotiation, make twice as much money, work half as hard and live to be 95. In return, the lawyer has to promise the devil the souls of his parents, his wife and his three young children.

The lawyer thinks for a moment, then asks, "So what's the catch?"

A hockey fan is driving home from work when he passes by a local priest. He stops and offers him a lift. The priest thanks him kindly and together they proceed to the church to drop the priest off.

On the way they pass a man walking his dog on the other side of the road; on closer inspection the driver realizes the pedestrian is NHL commissioner Gary Bettman. The driver hates the NHL boss and suddenly feels an uncontrollable urge to run Bettman over with his car. He puts his foot down on the accelerator and races toward him, but at the last minute Bettman jumps out of the way. The driver of the car hears a bang, but he is sure he missed Bettman.

> *Q: What did Gary Bettman say when the NHLPA asked him for more money?*
>
> *A: "Sorry, I'm a little short."*

The driver and the priest continue to the church in silence, and when the hockey fan pulls up, he says, "Look, Father, I'm really sorry about that incident back there. I don't know what came over me. Can you forgive me, Father?"

The priest replies, "Of course I can forgive you, my son. And don't worry, I got him with the car door."

Did you hear about the new doll called "Negotiation Bettman"? It comes with all the players' stuff.

In Good Company

Gary Bettman, Mario Lemieux and Wayne Gretzky all die and meet in heaven. God is sitting in his chair waiting for them. He says to the three legends, "Gentlemen before I let you in, you must tell me what you believe. Mario, we'll start with you. What do you believe?"

Lemieux replies, "I believe hockey is the greatest thing in the world and the best sport in history."

To that, God says, "Take the seat to my left." God then turns to Wayne and says, "Wayne, what do you believe?"

Gretzky replies, "I believe that to be the best, you've got to give every ounce you've got!"

To that, God says, "Take the seat to my right." God then turns to Bettman and says, "Gary, tell me, what do you believe?"

Bettman replies, "I believe you are sitting in my seat."

Two Kids on a Playground

Two small boys meet during their first day at school. "My name is Billy. What's yours?" asks the first boy.

"Tommy," replies the second.

"My daddy is an accountant," says Billy. "What does your daddy do?"

"My daddy is an NHL owner."

"Honest?" says Billy.

"No, just the normal kind," replies Tommy.

Johnny is in his fifth grade class when the teacher asks the children what their fathers do for a living. All the typical answers come up, such as fireman, policeman, salesman and the like. Johnny is uncharacteristically quiet, so the teacher asks him about his father.

Johnny says, "My father is an exotic dancer at a gay bar and takes his clothes off in front of other men. Sometimes, if the offer's really good, he'll go out to the alley with some guy and have sex with him for money."

The teacher, obviously shaken by his statement, hurriedly sets the other children to work on some assignment and takes Johnny aside. "Is that really true about your father?" she asks.

"Well, not really," says Johnny. "He is the NHL commissioner, but I am too embarrassed to say that in front of the other kids."

Carnac the Magnificent

Nobody knows that, a few years ago, spent some time with Carnac the Magnificent. He taught me the secrets of psychic prediction, but I was only ever able to master the art so long as it involved images that came in threes. Here, now, are two of my hockey-related psychic readings.

Each list of three items is followed by the thing that my amazing abilities have revealed ties them together.

1. Raw Steak
2. Fireworks
3. Gary Bettman

☛ **Three things that should be fired!**

1. Die Hard
2. Die Harder
3. Die Hard With a Vengeance

☛ **The last three lockouts.**

Did you hear that the Columbus Blue Jackets have a new owner? Yup, he's a billionaire from China. His name is Win Wun Soon.

Bettman's Answering Machine

The message on Gary Bettman's answering machine: "Hi! This is Gary! If you are my kids, I already sent the money. If you are an owner, settle this thing about the money. If you are the NHLPA, I don't have enough money. If you are my friends, you owe me money. If you are my wife, don't worry, I have plenty of money."

Q: What do you get when you cross a godfather with an NHL lawyer?

A: An offer you really can't understand.

NHL Chain Letter

This is a chain letter. Do not break the chain, or the National Hockey League will sue you and lock you out of your computer.

Hello. My name is Gary Bettman, and I am commissioner of a struggling hockey empire based in the village of New York in a remote nation called the United States of America (and, for now, in some parts of a border country called Canada, although we are trying to fix that). Survival is not easy in my empire. Often it gets very cold outside, forcing our officers to flee to warmer places, like Hawaii or Florida, to hold our winter survival meetings. Soon, we will run out of such places in our own country and will be forced to migrate to foreign places like the Costa del Sol.

Our plight grows more desperate by the day. Just this week, for instance, during a caviar break, I learned that our empire's revenues have trebled in the '90s to about $14 billion because of expansion fees and several other forms of highway robbery that do not actually involve the use of a gun. It was noted that the governments of our teams in the Canadian colonies are still refusing to grant their team tax privileges and other pork barrel sustenance not available to the common folk.

Frankly, we are halfway to our wits' end trying to convince them to open their hearts and wallets so that our empire can continue to grow and prosper without

Most Unnecessary Book Ever: *The Art of Negotiation by Gary Bettman*

forcing us to open our own. How can we make them understand our plight? Why can they not understand that, though revenues in the wealthier outposts are generally $60–70 million, the poorer must get by on merely $30–40 million?

Desperate, we turn to you for help. Please send this letter to five of your friends and ask each of them to send us $10 (U.S. funds; no coins or stamps). They must, of course, send copies to five of THEIR friends, with instructions to do the same thing.

We beg you not to turn your back on our people— not because it will hurt us but because dreadful things could happen to you. Only a few years ago, someone broke one of our earlier chains in Atlanta. Within months, their hockey outpost was blown clear to the frozen lands of someplace called Winterpeg. The people of Atlanta stood in the sweltering heat of Georgia and lamented the way they'd ignored the warnings from a Canadian place called Ke-Bec that had also broken the chain. The Ke-Bec legend is retold each year as our people gather 'round the liqueur table at our annual meetings: the Ke-Bec people watched one team disappear into Colorado.

Do not let this happen to you. Do not break the chain. Pick five of your richest friends and add links to our survival fund, named for one of our patron saints. Send all contributions to Fund Our Scam To Expand Revenue (FOSTER), NHL, New York. No receipts will be issued, so that we can save pennies otherwise wasted on stamps.

Hurry. We're running out of Champagne.

Signed,

Your humble servant, Gary Bettman

Boss Time

The irritable owner of the Boston Bruins, Jeremy Jacobs, had just concluded a meeting with the NHL board of directors. Sensing it hadn't gone well, he turns furiously on his hapless assistant and snarls, "Where the hell's my pen?"

"Why, it's behind your ear Mr. Jacobs," she says timidly.

"Goddamit, Brenda, you know how busy I am!" he yells back. "Which ear?"

Sign in the NHL board offices: THANK HEAVENS THIS IS A FREE COUNTRY WHERE YOU CAN DO EXACTLY AS THE LEAGUE PLEASES.

Captured

Gary Bettman, Jeremy Jacobs and Shane Doan are captured by an evil gang and are to be tortured with 50 lashes. The gang leader is in a good mood and allows the three hockey men the choice of something to put on their backs.

Q: How do you piss off Gary Bettman?
A: Give him a yo-yo.

"What do you want on your back, Bettman?" asks the gang leader.

"Nothing. I am not giving you the satisfaction of winning this negotiation," says the stubborn Bettman, and he receives his lashes with a slight smirk on his face.

"What do you want on your back, Jacobs?" asks the gang leader.

"Goalie pads," answers Jacobs, who feels none of the 50 lashes.

"What do you want on your back, Doan?" asks the leader.

"Bettman," answers Doan.

A Version of Charity

Gary Bettman wants very much to participate in charities to prove to the world that he is not a miserable, heartless, corporate suit. So when the Annual Easter Charity Ball for the homeless comes around, he volunteers to head the committee. It takes a lot of organization, but the party goes off without a hitch, and he dines and dances into the wee hours.

When the festivities end, he is upset to see a bag lady bundled on the sidewalk next to his Mercedes. Hearing the jingle of Bettman's keys, the old woman extends her grimy hand and asks Bettman if he can spare any change.

"Ohhh," gasps Bettman, "the nerve! And after I spent all night slaving to help you people. Aren't you ever satisfied?"

Public Relations Battle

This latest NHL lockout from 2012–13 was a public relations nightmare for both the National Hockey League and the players association. Fans of the game at the beginning of this mess were angry and looking for someone to string up by the neck. The most natural direction for their hatred was the owners and the league, but this time the NHL tried to change public opinion. This time they turned to Dr. Evil himself, a man named Frank Luntz.

Those of you who are into American politics will know this man well, or at least you will know his PR management style, because he is the genius behind the Republican Party and their constant attacks against everything rational, like health care reform and global warming, and a style of political language completely adopted by the Fox News Channel.

> **Q:** *How does Gary Bettman change a light bulb?*
>
> **A:** *He holds it in the air, and the world revolves around him.*

Frank Luntz makes a living by twisting words. He often likes to say, "Eighty percent of our life is emotion, and only 20 percent is intellect. I am much more interested in how you feel than how you think." It is his goal in life to take an event or idea and twist the words and meaning so that at the end of the day, you come out believing his side is 100 percent right and that you will defend it completely as the truth. He may be evil, but the man is good at his job.

That is why his public relations firm was approached by the NHL at the start of the lockout to pull together a focus group and test the many angles that the NHL and its owners could take in a possible media war with the players. The NHL realized early on that they are at a disadvantage when it comes to their public image. Without help, the players have a natural advantage in the publicity war given their already heroic status with the fans. But during this lockout the league sensed that things were different, that they had an opportunity to change public opinion in their favor. Bill Daly, deputy commissioner of the NHL, said in an interview with the *Minneapolis Star Tribune* that "Fan perception is important to us, but at the end of the day, we have to do an economic deal that's going to work for our clubs and our owners and our business, and that's going to make the league healthy going forward."

The NHL conducts market research fairly regularly, but this was a first for the league when it came to the lockout, and they turned to the best for help because, as Daly put forth himself, fan perception and a healthy league are tied together.

So to the Luntz Group the NHL went with the problem of how to market CBA negotiations to the public, and what they came up with was telling.

The NHL presented the PR focus group with a packet of information that laid out the problems of the CBA negotiations, and they were to choose the message that the NHL could use that sounded the nicest. The term that kept coming up most of the time was "shared sacrifice."

"Maybe we asked for too much at first," Luntz's mock-NHL speech went, "but we're willing to give. The NHLPA has to be willing to give as well, if we're going to give the fans back their hockey. There's no way we're going to do this without both sides bringing something to the table."

Shortest book ever: *How to Win Friends and Influence People* by Gary Bettman

The idea that came out was to portray the league as conciliatory and the players as the ones who were making unreasonable demands. It was a sneaky tactic, but Luntz has proved before that even the scientific fact that the earth is warming can be twisted. Surely NHL contract negotiations and revenue sharing can be skewed in one's favor.

All of this, however, was supposed to be a secret, and when the word was leaked courtesy an article via deadspin.com, the league tried to cover up their sneaky indiscretion as merely another one of its many focus groups.

Dance with the devil, NHL, and you're gonna get burned.

Removal

When negotiations between the NHL and the players association reached an impasse in late 2012, the two parties agreed to allow professional Federal U.S. mediators into the room to see if they could help salvage the process. Normally these individuals are ultra professional with years of boardroom and negotiation experience. They rise above the level of the petty problems that can interfere with a contract dispute so they can resolve a problem quickly and fairly.

> **Q:** *What do you call it when Gary Bettman blows in Bill Daly's ear?*
> **A:** *Data transfer.*

One of the mediators brought into the process on November 28, 2012, was a man named Guy Serota.

He came with glowing reviews and was, apparently, committed to the process of ending the lockout. Naturally the press and the public were curious about this mediator and turned to the Internet to see what they could find out about him. Well, they quickly found his Twitter account, and everything went downhill from there for Mr. Serota. It would seem that Serota thought posting strange things on Twitter would never return to bite him in the backside, but he was wrong. His account was filled with strange off-color jokes, and for some reason he especially did not like comedian Sarah Silverman, to whom he tweeted, "What does [the] fact Sarah is Jewish have to do with her being a terrorist whore? Racist! @SarahSilverman F*ck you to hell jew terrorist whore."

Just two hours after being assigned the position, Serota was removed from the case. He claimed that his account had been hacked by some unscrupulous malcontent, but the strange tweets had been occurring for weeks, so no one was buying his defense.

Without warning, a hurricane blows across the Caribbean. A luxurious yacht soon wanders into a huge wave and sinks without a trace. Only two survivors, the ship's captain and the boat's owner, New Jersey Devils owner Jeffrey Vanderbeek, manage to swim to the closest island. Observing that it is utterly uninhabited, the captain bursts

THE OWNERS, THE LEAGUE AND MR. BETTMAN   55

into tears, wringing his hands and moaning that they'll never be rescued. Meanwhile, his companion leans back against a palm tree and relaxes.

"Mr. Vanderbeek, how can you be so calm?" moans the distraught steward. "We're going to die on this godforsaken island. They're never going to find us."

"Let me tell you something," says Vanderbeek. "Two years ago I gave Travis Zajac, Martin Brodeur and Dainius Zubrus two-year multi-million dollar contracts."

"So, what's that got to do with us getting saved?" asks the fear-stricken captain.

"Well, their contracts are up, and there is one thing that is certain in this world. When a hockey player wants money, he will surely find you."

Customs

Boston Bruins owner Jeremy Jacobs dies suddenly. His heartbroken widow organizes the funeral and invites every one he knew. When the service is over, she asks his three closest friends to place an offering in the casket, as it was a family tradition.

Moved by her suffering, the first friend, another NHL owner, gently deposits $1000 in the coffin.

Wiping the tears away, the second friend, the Bruins general manager, puts $1500 on Jacobs' pillow.

His third friend, Gary Bettman, writes out a check for $4500, puts it in the casket and pockets the cash.

Two professional hockey players meet on the street.

"Man, it was cold this morning, eh!" says one player.

"How cold was it?" asks the other.

"I don't know exactly what the temperature was, but I saw Gary Bettman and the owners with their hands in their own pockets."

Negotiating Allegory

Gary Bettman is out fishing one day when he catches a strange-looking fish. He reels the fish in, unhooks it and throws it on the ground next to him. The fish starts writhing in agony and, to Bettman's surprise, says, "Please throw me back into the lake, and I'll grant you three wishes."

"Any three wishes, eh?" Bettman muses as visions of women, expensive houses and platform shoes dance through his head. "Fish," he says, "I'll do this. Give me five wishes and I'll throw you back."

"Sorry," answers the fish while struggling for breath, "only three wishes."

Bettman's pride is at stake, and after giving the matter some thought, he says, "What do you take me for? A sucker? I'll settle for four wishes."

"Only three," the fish says weakly.

Fuming, Bettman debates the pros and cons of accepting the three wishes or continuing to bargain for that one extra wish. Finally, Bettman decides it isn't worth looking a gift fish in the mouth. He says, "All right fish, you win, three wishes."

Unfortunately the fish is dead.

How the NHL Approaches CBA Negotiations

In the beginning was The Plan

And then came the Assumptions

And then the Assumptions were without form

And the Plan was completely without substance

And the darkness was upon the face of the players

And they spoke among themselves, saying,

"It's a crock of sh*t, and it stinketh to the highest of heaven."

And the players went unto their Union and sayeth,

"It is a pail of dung and none may abide the odor thereof."

And the Union went unto the Owners and sayeth unto them,

"It is a container of excrement and it is very strong, such that none may abide it."

And the Owners went unto the Board and sayeth,

"It is a vessel of fertilizer, and none are abiding its strength."

And the Board spoke among themselves, saying one to another,

"It contains that which aids plant growth, and it is very strong."

And the Board went unto the Deputy Commissioner and sayeth unto him,

"It promotes growth and is very powerful."

And the Deputy Commissioner went unto the Commissioner and sayeth unto him,

"This new plan will actively promote the growth and efficiency of this league and these areas in particular."

And the Commissioner looked upon the Plan

And saw that it was good, and The Plan became League Policy.

This is how sh*t happens.

Poor Bettman

A traffic cop finds Gary Bettman on the highway in a distressed state. With no money to pay his lawyers and convinced that his family hates him, he threatens to douse his clothes in gasoline and set himself on fire.

A passerby asks what is going on. The cop explains, adding that because he feels sorry for the

NHL commissioner, he is going from car to car asking for donations.

"How much have you collected so far?" asks the passerby.

"About 10 gallons."

Crash Landing

Gary Bettman, the Pope and a hippie are on board a small private plane when the pilot announces that they are in trouble and should bail out. Unfortunately, there are only two parachutes between the three passengers, meaning that someone will be left to face almost certain death. Before they can discuss it, Bettman snatches a parachute, runs for the door and jumps, screaming, "I'm far too important a person to die!"

The Pope and the hippie look at the one remaining parachute. The Pope says, "My son, I have lived a good, long life and I have faith that I will go to a better place. You take the last parachute."

"It's okay, you have it," says the hippie, reaching down. "I'll have this one. The NHL commissioner just jumped out with my backpack."

Three sharks meet in the ocean and talk about the people they've eaten recently. The first says, "I swallowed bin Laden yesterday, but the guy had eaten so much garlic I feel sick."

The second shark says, "I swallowed Vladimir Putin last week, but he had so much vodka in him that I'm still drunk."

The third shark says, "You're lucky. I swallowed Gary Bettman three weeks ago and the guy had so much air in his head that I still can't dive."

Life Saver

In the middle of lockout negotiations, Gary Bettman falls into a freezing lake in Canada and is rescued from drowning by three small boys. He is so grateful that he tells the boys, "I'll give you anything you want for saving my life."

The first boy thinks and says, "I'd like a Ferrari, red, and a million dollars."

"No problem," says Bettman. "You will have what you want. What about you, little boy?"

"I'd like to play hockey with Wayne Gretzky, Sidney Crosby and Martin Brodeur," says the second boy.

"Sure," says Bettman. "That I can do, no problem. How about you, my little hero?"

"I'd like a motorized wheelchair," says the third boy.

"Why would you need a wheelchair?" asks Bettman. "You look pretty healthy to me."

"Because," says the boy, "I'll need a wheelchair when my dad finds out I saved Gary Bettman from drowning and now the lockout is going to continue."

THE OWNERS, THE LEAGUE AND MR. BETTMAN

First Day as Commissioner

On his first morning in the NHL head offices, a young Gary Bettman begins sorting out his office. He is in the middle of arranging his desk when there is a knock at the door. Eager to show that he has made it in the world, he picks up the phone to look busy and calls out to the person at the door. "Come in."

A tradesman enters the office, but Bettman talks into the phone as if he were conducting important business. "I agree," he says. "Yes, yes…sure…no problem. You get that done right away and don't disappoint me." He hangs up. "Yes, can I help you?"

"Yes," replies the man. "I am here to hook up your phone."

Gary Bettman and two guys are standing on the roof of the Empire State Building. The first guy says, "You know, the winds here in New York are so strong that you could step off the edge of this building and literally float in mid-air because of the upward thrust of the thermal air current."

"You're crazy," says Bettman.

"You don't believe me?" says the first guy. "Watch this."

And with that, the first guy steps off the edge of the Empire State Building, floats around in mid-air and returns safely to the roof without a care.

"That was amazing," says Bettman. "I've got to try that."

And so Bettman steps off the edge of the Empire State Building. But instead of floating, he plummets like a stone down to the concrete below.

Seeing this, the third guy, who had remained silent until then, turns to the first guy and says, "You know something? There are times when you can be a real *sshole, Superman."

AHHH HA!

Negotiations between NHLPA members and the owners are at an impasse. The union denies that their players are flagrantly abusing their contracts' sick-leave provisions.

One morning at the bargaining table, the league's chief negotiator holds aloft the morning edition of the newspaper. "This man," he announces, "called in sick yesterday!"

There on the sports page is a photo of the supposedly ill player, who had just won a local golf tournament with an excellent score.

The silence in the room is broken by a union negotiator.

"Wow," he says. "Just think of what kind of score he could have had if he hadn't been sick!"

Stuck

A boy is playing with a coin when it gets stuck in his throat, and he starts to choke. His mother runs into the street calling for help, and a passing man offers his assistance. The man grabs hold of the boy, puts his mouth over the boy's mouth and skillfully sucks out the coin.

"Thank you, doctor," says the woman. "Did you learn that in medical school?"

"Oh, I'm not a doctor," replies the man. "I'm the NHL commissioner."

⤙ CHAPTER 4 ⤚

Hockey Fan Revolution

Being a fan of modern hockey has not been easy. In the past 20 years, there have been three lockouts, with one lasting an entire season. To say the fan of the NHL brand of hockey has been stressed out is to put it mildly.

Hockey fans are a unique bunch. They not only love their sport but they also live it. It is part of their identity. No other sport has such hardcore fans, and to put them through three work stoppages in less than 20 years was downright cruel. However, hockey fans are just as tough as the players they watch, and NHL fans have found thousands of ways to keep themselves occupied—some more ingenious than others, and some displaying true passion not for NHL hockey, but for the sport in general.

The Fight for the Return of the Challenge Cup

A long time ago, in a land far, far away, a silversmith hammered out a glorious-looking trophy commissioned by then Governor General of the Dominion of Canada, Lord Stanley of Preston. Lord Stanley decreed that said trophy was to be named the Dominion Hockey Challenge Cup and was to be awarded to the top amateur team in Canada, to be decided by the acceptance of a challenge from another team. Lord Stanley's five point

HOCKEY FAN REVOLUTION 65

rules for the awarding of the cup were simple enough.

1. The winners shall return the Cup in good order when required by the trustees so it may be handed over to any other team that may win it.

2. Each winning team, at its own expense, may have the club name and year engraved on a silver ring fitted on the Cup.

3. The Cup shall remain a challenge cup and should not become the property of one team, even if won more than once.

4. The trustees shall maintain absolute authority in all situations or disputes over the winner of the Cup.

5. If one of the existing trustees resigns or drops out, the remaining trustees shall nominate a substitute.

These rules were set in stone and followed as gospel for many years. But as time went on and the face of hockey changed along with North America, the awarding of the Stanley's Cup changed as well. It was this original decree, especially the third part, that many fans during the 2004–05 lockout pointed too when they legally challenged the NHL's right to hold onto the Stanley Cup. When Gary Bettman announced in January of 2005 that the league and the players could not come to an agreement, a group of Toronto beer league hockey players banded together and sought out the advice of a Toronto-based lawyer named Tim Gilbert.

"We kind of felt that, given [the NHL] acknowledged that there's a trust, and the trustees are the ones who have responsibility to administer the trust, we can't bind their hands and tell them exactly what to do," said Gilbert, who led the case for the recreational players. "But they have to exercise their duties in the best interests of the original purpose of the trust, which was to promote hockey."

So the beer leaguers and their lawyer took their challenge and filed a claim with the Ontario Supreme Court, and in 2006, they won. Sort of. The decision gave the Stanley Cup trustees the opportunity—but not the obligation—to "award the Stanley Cup to a non-NHL team in any year in which the NHL fails to organize a competition to determine a Stanley Cup winner."

This decision may have pleased beer leaguers across Canada and the United States who had dreamed of lifting the Cup since they were kids, but in reality, the court ruling was completely in the NHL's favor. The board of trustees of the Stanley Cup would never give the Cup to a team in any league other than the NHL.

"The chances of both Brian (O'Neil) and I agreeing that it should go to any group that plays for it,

Note to Fans: Wearing a jersey when there is no hockey looks stupid. It's easy to get used to looking like you belong to a certain team, but without any point of reference, the non-hockey watching minority will probably just think you like Kevin Smith movies. Or worse, Kevin Smith.

I wouldn't hold your breath," said fellow trustee Ian (Scotty) Morrison, who also serves on the board for the Hockey Hall of Fame, in a *National Post* interview.

But the legal battle did accomplish one amazing thing. It got the NHL to admit that it was not the owner of the Stanley Cup! And, yes, they agreed to donate $500,000 to a program run by Hockey Canada to promote the game to young women and underprivileged children.

So despite a legal battle and a stunning admission from the league, Lord Stanley's Cup has not been out of the NHL's control since 1926. The last non-NHL team to win the Cup was the 1925 Victoria Cougars of the Western Canadian Hockey League.

The thought of the Stanley Cup getting handed over to an amateur club sounds like a rational idea if the NHL can't get its act together, but when the Governor General Lord Stanley first envisioned the trophy, there were only a handful of teams playing amateur hockey, under gas lights on outdoor rinks. One hundred years later the game has changed, and the Cup is no longer the Dominion Challenge Cup, it's the Stanley fricken Cup! The Holy Grail of Hockey. You cannot simply hand it over to some beer leaguer named Bob who plays only on Saturday nights and is most often half in the bag on Molson's when he is on the ice. The trustees know that the Stanley Cup is intended to be handed out to the best players in the world and, like it or not, those players reside within the National Hockey League.

Gary at the Gun Range

Canadians get frustrated when there is no hockey. Normally Canadians take disappointment with a quiet reserve that is famous around the globe; however, when someone dares to take away their hockey, all bets are off.

Some gun-toting Port Coquitlam, BC, hockey fans decided to take their frustrations over the lockout down to the local gun range and empty a few thousand rounds into a cartoon picture of NHL commissioner Gary Bettman.

The poster featured a big-eared picture of Bettman surrounded by targets with a line that read, "Let us express how we feel about the lockout."

The manager of the gun range said that gun aficionados can bring their own targets down to the range, and since the lockout, Gary Bettman has definitely been the target of choice. Prior to that, Justin Bieber was the favorite target of the trigger happy. Of the Bettman poster, the gun range owner, Wes Yen, said, "He probably equals the zombie targets that we sell…. It's good for my business. When there's nothing on TV, people will come down to the range and start shooting."

Things You Will Never Hear Fans Say During an NHL Lockout

- Those poor players. I hope they can pay their bills.
- I think deep down Bettman is a sweetheart.
- You know, I would just love to sit down and have a beer with Donald Fehr and Gary Bettman and tell them that love conquers all.
- I miss watching the Phoenix Coyotes.
- The players should be making more money.
- This was the Leafs' year to win the Cup.
- Hey guys, check it out! I just got Peterborough Petes season tickets!
- I'm so glad Carrie Underwood and Mike Fisher have time to spend together as husband and wife.
- Thank goodness hockey is gone. Now I can watch more cricket.
- Yay! Now my girlfriend and I can spend Saturday nights on the couch watching *Sex and the City* on DVD instead of *Hockey Night in Canada*.
- I'm going to sign up for the Russian Kontinental Hockey League (KHL) fan club.
- Peewee hockey is where it's at!
- I prefer table top hockey, anyway.
- Tell me more about revenue sharing.
- These Russian KHL players are all about teamwork.
- I wonder what Ovechkin is up to.
- I finally have the time to take up knitting.

Lockout Injury

Andy comes to work one day, limping something awful. One of his co-workers, Josh, notices and asks Andy what happened.

Andy replies, "Oh, nothing. It's just an old hockey injury that acts up once in a while."

"Gee, I never knew you played hockey," says Josh.

Andy replies, "I don't. I hurt it last year when Bettman announced another lockout. I put my foot through the television."

What Men and Women Want

What Women Want: To be loved, to be listened to, to be desired, to be respected, to be needed, to be trusted and, sometimes, just to be held.

What Men Want: No more lockouts.

Three guys are sitting behind three nuns at the first NHL game back from the lockout. The men decide to antagonize the nuns to get them to move. So the first guy says to the others (loud enough for the women ahead to hear), "I think I want to move to Montreal. There are only 100 Catholics living there."

The second guy speaks up and says, "I want to move to Edmonton. Only 50 Catholics live there."

The third guy speaks up and says, "I want to move to Toronto. There are only 25 Catholics living there."

One of the nuns turns around, looks the third guy in the eye and calmly says, "Why don't you go to hell? There aren't any Catholics there."

Fan Love?

On a tour of Florida, the Pope takes a couple of days off his itinerary to visit the coastline on an impromptu sightseeing trip. He is driving his 4x4 Popemobile along the beautiful shoreline in an area where Canadian tourists typically visit when he hears an enormous commotion just off the headland. He drives closer to see what is going on. As he approaches the scene, he sees a man in the water wearing a Boston Bruins hockey jersey struggling frantically to free himself from the jaws of a 25-foot shark. At that moment, a speedboat containing three men wearing Montreal Canadiens jerseys roars into view from around the point. One of the men takes aim and fires a harpoon into the shark's ribs, immobilizing it instantly. The other two men reach out and pull the bleeding, semi-conscious Bruins fan from the water and then, using long clubs, beat the shark to death and pull it into the boat. As they prepare for a hasty retreat, they hear frantic shouting from the shore. It is the Pope summoning them to the beach. When they reach shore, the Pope praises them for the rescue.

"I give you my blessing for your brave actions," he says. "I had heard that there was bitter hatred between the fans of the Canadiens and the Bruins, but now I have seen with my own eyes this is not true. I can see that your society is an enlightened example of true harmony, and your compassion could serve as a model for other countries, like this one, to follow." He blesses them all and drives off in a cloud of dust.

As he departs, the harpooner asks the others, "Who was that?"

"That," one guy answers, "was His Holiness, the Pope. He is in direct contact with God and has access to all of God's wisdom."

"Well," the harpooner says, "he doesn't know a thing about shark fishing. Now, is the bait holding up okay, or do we need to get another one?"

You Know You're a Hockey Fan if...

- Your idea of serving breakfast is giving each of your kids a fork and dropping an Eggo in the middle of the table.
- You punish your kids with "minors," "majors" and "misconducts."
- When you come to a traffic signal and the light turns red, you get really excited and start cheering.
- You consider the Forum in Montreal a place of worship.
- You keep a picture of the Stanley Cup in your wallet in front of the picture of your family.

HOCKEY FAN REVOLUTION   73

- Instead of duct tape, you use hockey tape to fix everything.
- You know the difference between "The Garden," "The Gahden" and "The Gardens."
- You call a trip to the Hockey Hall of Fame a "pilgrimage."
- You send Gordie Howe a birthday card, yet you can't even remember your own family members' birthdays.
- Your kids are named Gordie, Bobby and Wayne.
- You went to see *West Side Story* because you thought it was about a game between Winnipeg and San Jose.
- You went into a bank because it advertised "Free Checking"… and walked out disappointed.
- When someone refers to "The Classics," you think they're talking about the Original Six.
- Your cure for everything is a couple extra-strength aspirin and a shot of Novocain.
- You can pronounce anything in French, yet you have no idea what it means.
- Every time you hear a siren, you wonder who scored.
- You can say "Khabibulin," "Tkachuk," "Jagr," "Leschyshyn" and "Nikolishin" without getting tongue-tied.
- Every time you see the name "Roy" you automatically pronounce it *Wah*.
- You're not allowed to play chess simply because the first time you played, you misunderstood the meaning of the word "check."
- You think the four food groups are nachos, beer, pretzels and rubber.
- Everything in your wardrobe is your team's colors.

- You still remember which teams were in the Patrick, Smythe, Norris and Adams divisions and which divisions were in the Campbell and Prince of Wales conferences.
- You know the difference between "The Edmonton Express" and "The Human Express."
- You refer to your team's enforcers as "chippy players" and you refer to other teams' enforcers as "freaking little pieces of monkey sh*t."
- When you're at a game, you're not bothered when your kid says "F**k!" but when he says "shutout" before the game is over, you threaten to wash his mouth out with soap.
- You wonder what Miroslav Satan did to become the Prince of Darkness and Ruler of Hell.
- You think the proper way to spell the plural of "leaf" is "leafs."
- Every time an NHL lockout occurs, you return an even bigger fan, despite hating them for it.
- You find stitches and broken noses attractive.
- You only watch the hockey parts of *Happy Gilmore.*
- You think there are three periods in a basketball game.
- You show up at games three hours early.
- You cried when Wayne Gretzky retired.
- You buy season tickets even though you can't afford them.
- You refer to every player on the roster by his nickname and know every pre-game ritual.
- You use a hockey puck as a paperweight.
- You consider taking your vacation time to attend every All-Star Weekend within reach.

- You consider body checking obnoxious customers at work when they ask stupid questions.
- You aren't ashamed to admit that you've seen all the Mighty Ducks movies and can recite key parts ("Goalie's bored, Fulton scored...").
- You know which referees are biased against your team.
- You are planning road trips for away games, and the schedule isn't out yet.

Hockey's Back

A man is flipping through channels on his TV and narrows his decision down to two, one featuring a lusty couple in a dirty movie and another the first hockey game back from the lockout.

"I don't know whether to watch them or the game," he says to his wife.

"For heaven's sake, watch them," his wife responds. "You already know how to play hockey!"

A disgruntled hockey fan angry about the lockout appears in court charged with disorderly conduct and assault. The arresting officer, giving evidence, states that the accused threw something into the canal.

"What exactly was it that he threw?" asks the magistrate.

"Stones, sir."

"Well, that's hardly an offense is it?"

"It was in this case, sir," says the police officer. "Stones is an NHL lawyer."

Doctor's Appointment

An exhausted looking Montreal Canadiens fan drags himself into the doctor's office. "Doctor, there are dogs all over my neighborhood. They bark all day and all night, and I can't get a wink of sleep."

"I have good news for you," the doctor answers, rummaging through a drawer full of sample medications. "Here are some new sleeping pills that work like a dream. A few of these, and your trouble will be over."

"Great," the Canadiens fan answers. "I'll try anything. Let's give it a shot."

A few weeks later the Canadiens fan returns, looking worse than ever. "Doc, your plan is no good. I'm more tired than before!"

"I don't understand how that could be," says the doctor, shaking his head. "Those are the strongest pills on the market!"

"That may be true," answers the Canadiens fan wearily, "but I'm still up all night chasing those dogs, and when I finally catch one, it's hard getting him to swallow the pill!"

Without Hockey, Fans Drink Too Much

A guy comes home completely drunk one night. He lurches through the door and is met by his scowling wife, who is definitely not happy. "Where the hell have you been all night?" she demands.

"With no hockey on, I just couldn't go to my usual sports bar. I found this fantastic new place," he says. "The Golden Saloon. Everything there is golden. It's got huge golden doors, a golden floor, the works—hell, even the urinal's gold!"

The wife doesn't believe his story, and the next day she checks the phone book, finding a place across town called the Golden Saloon. She calls up the place to check her husband's story.

"Is this the Golden Saloon?" she asks when the bartender answers the phone.

"Yes, it is," the bartender answers.

"Do you have huge golden doors?"

"Sure do."

"Do you have golden floors?"

"Most certainly do."

"What about golden urinals?"

There's a long pause, then the woman hears the bartender yelling, "Hey, Duke, I think I got a lead on the guy that pissed in your saxophone last night!"

I hate it when my wife wears my Leafs jersey to bed. It's her way of telling me it's going to be another night without scoring.

At the Gates

A man knocks on the Pearly Gates. His face is old, and his clothes are stained. He trembles and shakes with fear as St. Peter says, "What have you done to gain admission here?"

"Sir, I've been a loyal fan of the NHL all my life," says the man.

The Pearly Gates suddenly swing open. "Come in and choose your harp, angel," St. Peter says. "You've had your share of hell."

Pickup Game

With no hockey on TV, a group of hockey players from Montreal plays a pickup game against a team from a local monastery. Just before the game, the other team, all of whom are monks, kneel solemnly on the ice, put their hands together and indulge in five minutes of silent prayer. The monastery then trounces their hosts 13–1. After the match, the Montreal captain says, "Well boys, we've been out-played before, but this is the first time we've ever been out-prayed."

My American Wife

As in many Canadian homes on New Year's Eve, my wife and I face the annual conflict over what is more important: the World Junior Championship hockey games on TV or New Year's Eve dinner. To keep the peace, I eat dinner with the rest of the family and even linger for some pleasant after-dinner conversation before retiring to the family room to turn on the game. Several minutes later, my wife comes downstairs and graciously brings me a cold drink. She smiles, kisses me on the cheek and asks what the score is. I tell her it is the end of the second period and that the score is still nothing to nothing. "See?" she says. "You didn't miss a thing."

Dear Abby,

I have never written to you before, but I really need your advice. I suspect that my wife has been cheating on me. The usual signs are all there: the phone rings but if I answer, the caller hangs up; my wife goes out with "the girls" a lot but when I ask their names, she always says, "Just some friends from work. You don't know them." I try to stay awake and look out for her when she comes home, but I usually fall asleep. Anyway, I have not broached the subject with my wife. I think deep down I just did not want to know the truth, but last night she went out again and I decided to finally check on her.

Around midnight, I hid in the garage behind my hockey equipment so I could get a good view of the whole street when she arrived home. When she got out of the car she was buttoning up her blouse, and she took her panties out of her purse and slipped them on. It was at that moment, crouching behind my hockey gear, that I noticed a hairline crack where the blade meets the graphite shaft on my new one-piece hockey stick. Is this something I can fix myself or should I take it back to the pro-shop where I bought it?

Signed,

Hockey Fan

"My wife is like the hockey lockout," one man says to another. "I haven't scored for months."

Hockey Heaven

Two old guys are sitting in Tim Hortons after their seniors hockey game. One asks the other if he thinks there will be hockey in heaven. The friends make a promise to each other that the first to die will somehow let the other one know. A week later, one of the men dies. The following week, his friend recognizes his voice coming down from the heavens.

"Joe, I've got some good news and some bad news," says the disembodied voice. "The good news is that there is a hockey team in heaven.

They pull in thousands of fans every night, and you get to play with all the greats. Last night, Maurice Richard assisted me on five goals. The bad news is that you're starting in goal on Friday."

Do Me a Favor?

A young executive for the Montreal Canadiens arrives at a fancy restaurant in Toronto for a business meeting. He spots Gary Bettman at the restaurant bar and decides to approach him.

"Excuse me for interrupting your drink, Mr. Bettman," he says, "but I know how much you appreciate enterprise and initiative. I'm trying to win over a very important account today—it could really help if, while I am sitting with my client, you came by and said, 'Hey, Mike.' It would be an incredible favor, and I would make it up to you one day."

"Okay, no problem," sighs Bettman and returns to his drink. Later, as he's putting on his coat to leave, he remembers the young man's request. Obligingly he goes over to the man's table, taps him on the shoulder and says, "Hi, Mike."

"Get lost, Gary," snaps the young man. "Can't you see I'm busy!"

A passionate hockey fan is sitting in a window seat on a plane headed to New York. Just before take-off, he notices a man in a beautiful $3000 suit and realizes that it is Gary Bettman. Bettman walks over to where the hockey fan is sitting and happens to sit right next to him. They exchange glances, and a few minutes later the plane takes off. All is well for the moment. But then, the hockey fan realizes he needs to go to the bathroom, and Gary Bettman is fast asleep in his seat. The fan doesn't want to wake Bettman, so he decides to hold it in and wait for the sleeping man to wake up.

After a while the hockey fan starts to feel nauseated as well. He tries and tries to hold it in but then—*baaaarrrrffffffff!!!!*—he throws up all over Bettman and his $3000 suit. He thinks, *Oh no! He's going to sue me, or even worse, cause more lockouts.* So he sits there just waiting for Bettman to wake up.

Finally, Bettman slowly opens his eyes and finds vomit all over him. The hockey fan turns to him and says, "Well, do you feel better now?"

For the Love of Hockey

Two Canadian friends are avid hockey players, and every Thursday for many winters they have gone down to the local rink to shoot the puck around together. On the way to the rink, along a back road, they have to pass a cemetery.

One day as they approach the cemetery, a funeral is in progress, and one of the old friends stops, removes his hat and salutes the funeral.

"Hey," says the other friend, "in all these years we have been playing together, you've never once saluted any of the funerals we passed along the way."

"That's true, eh," replies his friend. "But when you've been married to a woman for 40 years, she's entitled to a bit of respect."

Overheard in a vegetarian restaurant: "I don't eat anything that has intelligence. On that note, I would gladly eat a hockey player."

Without Hockey, Canadians Are Filling the Void with Other Things

- They are finally giving lacrosse a chance as the other national sport.
- The church has seen a 25 percent increase in attendance just for the organ music.
- Some fans are just sitting in front of a blank TV on Saturday nights, yelling at the screen and calling Don Cherry an idiot.
- 50 percent of Canadians are trying to blow up Gary Bettman's head with their minds.
- Is it World Junior Championship time yet?
- Ugh. Watching KHL hockey.
- Parents are interviewing their kids after pee-wee games.

Top 10 Reasons Fans Should Not Forgive the NHL or the Players

10. Three lockouts in less than 20 years!

9. Ticket prices keep getting higher.

8. Gary Bettman is still the NHL boss.

7. The NHL has made billions of dollars, and the fans keep getting asked to buy more, pay more.

6. Cities that don't give a damn about hockey have teams (I'm talking to you New Jersey, Carolina and Florida) and cities that would die to have a team (Quebec, Hamilton) have nothing.

5. Ovechkin makes more than you do in five years and he still can't score!

4. I had to watch basketball to get my sports fix. BASKETBALL!

3. Guys had nothing to talk about for months at bars.

2. Romantic Comedy night! We had to sit through the same bloody movie plot over and over again.

1. This was my year to win the hockey pool!

House of Ill Repute

Gary Bettman decides he needs to get laid after all those CBA negotiations. Going to a high-class whorehouse, he finds a blonde, a redhead and a brunette waiting in the downstairs lounge. "I'm the commissioner of the National Hockey League," he says to the blonde. "How much will it cost me to spend a little time with you?"

HOCKEY FAN REVOLUTION

"Three hundred dollars," she says.

To the redhead, he poses the same question.

She replies, "Four hundred."

He makes the same proposition to the brunette.

She replies, "Mr. Commissioner, if you can raise my skirt as high as ticket prices, lower my panties as far as you have lowered the class in the game, get your penis as hard as a puck, keep it hard for as long as we waited for hockey in the last lockout and screw me like you did every fan of the game, then believe me, it isn't going to cost you a dime."

A Carolina Hurricanes fan is walking down the street in Toronto when he sees NHL commissioner Gary Bettman and asks, "Excuse me, but where's the Hockey Hall of Fame at?"

Bettman looks down his nose at the Carolina fan and replies haughtily, "Well, sir, did you learn nothing in school? You never end a sentence with a preposition."

"I'm sorry, Mister Bettman," says the fan sarcastically. "Where's the Hall of Fame at, *sshole."

Poor Hockey Wife

Frank's topics of conversation have always been limited to work and sports, and now that he's retired, he spends every waking minute attending games, glued to TSN or reading hockey blogs for

> **Q:** *How many Canadians does it take to screw in a light bulb?*
>
> **A:** *No one knows. They are all too busy playing hockey to care about some stupid light bulb.*

the latest rumors. At first, his wife, Kendra, was glad he had a hobby to keep him busy, but his obsession grew irritating and eventually maddening.

One night as they lay in bed together, Frank raptly watching a game pitting the Canadiens versus the Maple Leafs, Kendra decides she's had enough. She gets up, walks across the room and unplugs the television.

"Hey, what do you think you're doing?" protests Frank.

"Listen to me, Frank," she says. "I'm sick of sports. You've barely talked to me in weeks, not to mention actually touching me, and since the damn Canadiens came back from the lockout, you've been a zombie. It's time to talk about sex!"

"Uh, okay," replies Frank. "So how often do you think Carey Price gets laid?"

You Know You Play Too Much Hockey When...

- You body check the mailman.
- You call the referee whenever there is an argument.
- Instead of fighting the guy who stole your girlfriend, you challenge him to a game of floor hockey.

Top 10 Things Carolinians Do Instead of Watching Hockey

10. Visit Michael Jordan's hometown.

9. Watch their *Hee-Haw* tape collection.

8. Argue over whether Dale Earnhardt is better than Mark Martin.

7. Abuse tourists heading from New England to Florida.

6. Have sex with relatives.

5. Enter tobacco spitting contests.

4. Chase revenuers away from their stills.

3. Brush their tooth.

2. Brag about their college basketball teams.

1. Compare tattoo infections.

Two Combatants

Two guys are walking outside the Bell Centre in Montreal after a game between the Toronto Maple Leafs and the Montreal Canadiens, when they come across a Maple Leafs fan lying dead in the ditch. Just then, they hear a groan from across the street and rush over to find a badly wounded Montreal Canadiens fan. As they bend down to help him, they ask what happened.

He says, "I was face to face with the Leafs fan, right in the middle of the road, arguing about who had the better team. The tension was mounting. He said, 'The Canadiens are the worst team ever.' Then I said, 'Brian Burke ruined your team.' We were still shaking hands when the truck hit us."

Passionate Fan

After spending all day watching hockey on TV, a man falls asleep in his chair. His wife wakes him in the middle of the night. "It's ten to two," she says.

"For who?"

Just Drop It

When you mess with hockey, you mess with Canadians. Steve Chase, originally from Montreal and now living in Los Angeles, had enough of the league and the players fighting over the fans' money and the fans having no say in any of the debate. Talking about the lockout with a few of his expatriate pals after their weekly pickup game, they decided to voice their opinion by creating a video, and what came out of it was the "Just Drop It" movement. Other Internet-savvy hockey fans had tried to create a fan-based movement, but none had the success of the "Just Drop It" video.

The "Just Drop It" mantra is as follows, as taken from their Facebook page:

"Here's how it works: For every NHL game canceled after December 21st, we will boycott a game.

As an example, if we lose 10 games, then they'll lose the first 10 games when they return—we'll refrain from watching it on TV, from going to a game, and from buying any merchandise for the duration of the ban. We will keep track of this for you on our Facebook page. This is an effective way for the loyal fans—who make the sport possible in the first place—to be heard. If enough of us do this, we will get some measure of respect from the league and the union. Perhaps they'll find this movement amusing, but they'd be wise to not underestimate us!

> **Q:** *What do you call a woman who knows where her hockey-obsessed husband is every night?*
>
> **A:** *A widow.*

The Pledge: I pledge that for every game you take from me after December 21, I will refrain from attending any games, watching games on TV, and from buying any merchandise for the equivalent number of games after the lockout ends. You cancel one game...I'll take one from you. You take 20 from me...I'll skip the next 20...."

Steve Chase and his friends hoped to get a little traction with their video, but they quickly had several thousand supporters liking their page. Millions more who saw their video or the subsequent news reports began contemplating some sort of action to tell the league and the players that they'd had enough.

It was a good idea to show the NHL that the fans were not to be taken for granted, but the reality of the situation was that, though most fans took the idea seriously, the moment the return of hockey was announced and the players began hitting the ice for practice, the idea of a boycott quickly fell from fans' minds. Canadians, after all, are easy when it comes to hockey.

The Girl Who Wouldn't Shave

When it comes to hockey, it is usually the guys that do the most stupid things to prove their loyalty to the game and their teams. Men across North America love to show solidarity with their teams come playoff time by growing playoff beards. But without hockey, displays of love for one's team or the sport went silent. Paul Bissonnette of the Coyotes tweeted during the lockout that the players should all think about growing lockout beards in protest. Some guys out there probably did that, but what about the ladies who love hockey, too? What could they do to show support for their favorite sport? Well, 17-year-old Maggie Wagner of Ohio, a die-hard Pittsburgh Penguins fan, decided that although she could not grow a beard (thank god!), she would show her support for hockey and raise awareness in her town by not shaving her legs. So on September 15, the first official day of the lockout, she made a vow not too shave her legs until the lockout ended. By mid-October, her Twitter photos showed she had stuck to her word.

Q: Why are the Vancouver Canucks like Canada Post?

A: They both wear uniforms and don't deliver!

Her hairy gams were proudly displayed across the Internet and even got the attention of a few locked out NHLers, among them Dustin Penner, who suggested she wear pants on New Years Eve to at least give others a break from having to look at her legs. After more than 110 days of being locked out, those around her were very glad when hockey finally returned.

> *Q: How many NHL executives does it take to change a light bulb?*
>
> *A: None, they'll only promise change.*

CHAPTER 5
Our Favorite Teams

As fans of hockey, we enjoy the game for what it is, but it is made much better when you follow a team. Despite the many ups and downs of that particular squad, you stick with them. For some fans that means years of disappointment, anger and yelling at the TV, but they stubbornly stick with their club hoping and praying that the players can bring home the Stanley Cup. With the lockouts that have occurred over the years, it is not just the players, fans and owners that are affected—the teams themselves have suffered. Would the New Jersey Devils have won the Cup in 1995 had it been a full season? Could the Washington Capitals have won the Cup in 2004–05? Could the Leafs have made the playoffs? Would the Quebec Nordiques and the Winnipeg Jets still be around had the first lockout not occurred? These questions cannot be answered and they plague fans in the cities affect by the lockouts.

> Today, the National Hockey League announced the end of a 300-day lockout. Yeah, that is the best news for a Canadian since Celine Dion moved to Las Vegas.
>
> –Conan O'Brien, talk show host on the 2004–05 lockout

Better at Sex

A Senators fan and a Flyers fan are both madly in love with the same woman. The woman proposes a challenge: whoever can please her more during sex will be her boyfriend. Both men accept the challenge. That night, the woman she goes to bed with the Senators fan, and the following night she has sex with the Flyers fan. Afteward, she chooses the Flyers fan to be her boyfriend. Shocked and outraged, the Senators fan asks why she didn't choose him. She replies, "You, like your team, not only come up short but always finish early."

News Flash: This just in! Despite the lockout, the Buffalo Sabres somehow missed the playoffs again.

News Flash: This just in! The Los Angeles Kings will reportedly scale back ad buys for their 2012–13 local marketing campaign entitled, "Hey, Los Angeles, remember that hockey team you were a huge fan of for a few weeks last spring? No? Okay, didn't think so. Sorry to have bothered you."

New Team Dilemma

As a result of the lockout, the NHL is looking into adding more teams in Canada. They are considering giving a team to Hamilton, but Toronto is blocking the deal because they want a real team, too.

In Days of Yore

The last time the Toronto Maple Leafs won the Cup...

- The number one song on the Billboard charts was "Whiter Shade of Pale" by Procol Harum.
- Lyndon B. Johnson was *Time's* Man of the Year.
- The first handheld calculator was invented.
- *Rolling Stone* magazine printed its first issue.
- *In the Heat of the Night* won Best Picture at the Oscars.
- *The Andy Griffiths* was the most popular show on TV.
- Universal Medicare came into effect in Canada.
- Queen Elizabeth was 41 years old.
- Lester B. Pearson was Prime Minister of Canada.
- Curtis Joseph (aka Cujo) was born, as was Pamela Anderson.
- Charles de Gaulle gave his famous "Vive le Quebec Libre!" speech in Montreal.
- Che Guevara was killed in Bolivia.

To drum up interest in the Phoenix Coyotes, the NHL is giving away free tickets at the state's retirement homes.

Amazing Dog

A guy walks into a bar with his pet dog. The bartender says, "Sorry. No pets allowed."

The man replies, "This is a special dog. Turn on the Leafs game and you'll see." The bartender, curious to see what will happen, turns on the game.

The guy says, "Watch. Whenever the Leafs score, my dog does flips." The Leafs keep scoring, and the dog keeps flipping and jumping.

"Wow! That's one hell of a dog you got there. What happens when the Leafs actually win a game?"

The man replies, "I don't know. I've only had him for seven years."

"We've got the best hockey team in the country, unbeaten and no goals scored against us!"

"How many games have you played?"

"None, it's a lockout season."

For Love of the Teams

Four hockey fans are climbing a mountain. Each man is a fan of a different team, and as they climb higher, they argue about who is the most loyal to their team.

They continue to argue all the way up the mountain, and finally as they reach the top, the Canadiens fan hurls himself off the mountain, shouting, "This is for the great Montreal Canadiens!" as he falls to his doom.

Not wanting to be outdone, the Edmonton Oilers fan throws himself off the mountain, shouting "This is for the Oilers!"

Seeing this, the Ottawa Senators fan walks over to the edge and shouts, "This is for everyone!" and pushs the Toronto Maple Leafs fan off the side of the mountain.

> **Q:** *How do you spot a fake playoff ticket?*
> **A:** *It contains the word "Columbus."*

On the Move

News Flash: This just in! The Columbus Blue Jackets have been sold because of the lockout and have been moved to Kingston, Jamaica, where they will be renamed the Kingston Marijuana Leafs.

The Toronto Maple Leafs have apparently set up a call center for fans who are troubled by their current form. The number is 1-800-510-1010. Calls are charged at peak rate for overseas users. Once again that number is 1-800 five won nothing won nothing won nothing.

New Rules for Owning an NHL Franchise

- You must choose a color that the rest of the league will hate (not including the mandatory pink!), and you must choose a team name that is offensive to all cultural groups.

- The city must be located in a region that does not receive any ice or snow. Otherwise, the team will be fined $100 million for every inch of snow that falls.

- Do not attempt to place a team in Canada, or you will make Gary Bettman cry. He will sue you for enough money to create another team in a warm-climate city where nobody has ever heard of hockey.

- The only way to place a team in Canada is to first set it up in Atlanta. Then, after a few years of failure and obscurity, it can be moved to a Canadian city. At this point, it is optional whether to keep the current team name, or rename the team.

- You must be hazed by all the other owners and then sign an agreement not to talk about what happened in the hazing.

Robbed

The Detroit Red Wings return to where they parked in the Joe Louis Arena parking lot only to find that the people of Detroit had stripped the car bare and sold its parts to buyers in China and India.

How NHL Teams are Trying to Placate Fans After the 2012–13 Lockout

Let's face it, the NHL really screwed up and made a hell of a lot of fans angry. So to get them back, teams across the league are trying a variety of ways to appease the great anger of the hockey fans and get them spending their hard-earned dollars on NHL teams again. The following are strategies a few teams are trying to put butts back in the arenas.

> Did you hear that the Flames just hired a new Russian coach? I heard his name was Teedoff!

Los Angeles Kings: A shock and awe television and radio campaign will be implemented to remind people that all that fuss in June 2012 was not the result of the filming of a Michael Bay movie, that the people of Los Angeles do actually have a hockey team and it didn't leave when Gretzky left, and that they are in fact Stanley Cup champions.

Minnesota Wild: Fans that come back to games will be lucky enough to get punched in the gut by Ryan Suter and then mugged by Zach Parise. How else are they going to pay these guys?

Montreal Canadiens: Every fan will be allowed to slap PK Subban. Yes, yes, he's good, but don't you just want to smack him sometimes? Montrealers do.

Toronto Maple Leafs: To enhance the fans' experience, one unlucky fan will be selected at random and given the job of the Leafs general manager, and any trades that they make will be enforced. (Miraculously this works and the Leafs win the Cup.)

Winnipeg Jets: The first 5000 fans will receive free season tickets, because any Jets fan who is willing to leave their house in the middle of winter while living in the coldest place on earth deserves a few perks.

New Jersey Devils: Owners will drive bandwagons around the city on the day of the games and give free entrance to those that jump on.

Calgary Flames: General manager Jay Feaster will be handing out his secret donut recipe to all fans. *Mmmmm*, donuts.

New York Rangers: There will be a raffle before each game, and one lucky fan every game will have the chance to ask head coach John Tortorella one question during the post game press conference and get told to f*ck off.

With the NHL in lockout, a Chinese billionaire has started his own league in Beijing. The first team is called the Beijing Red Wongs.

Florida Panthers: One thousand lucky fans will get the privilege of hanging out with the players on the beaches of Miami after every game. Because everyone knows that the only reason players sign in Florida is for the beaches.

Penguins vs. Flyers

A Penguins fan, a Flyers fan and Pamela Anderson are sitting together on a train. The train enters a tunnel and the car goes completely dark. There's a kissing noise followed by the sound of a really loud slap. When the train comes out of the tunnel, Pamela Anderson and the Flyers fan are sitting as if nothing happened, and the Penguins fan is holding his slapped face. The Penguins fan is thinking, *That Flyers fan must have kissed Pamela, and she swung at him and missed, slapping me instead.* Pamela is thinking, *That Penguins fan must have tried to kiss me, accidentally kissed the Flyers fan, and got slapped for it.* And the Flyers fan is thinking, *This is great. The next time the train goes through a tunnel, I'll make another kissing noise and slap that Penguins fan again.*

> Did you hear that the Toronto Maple Leafs have a new area code all to themselves? It's 0-8-5.

Albert Einstein arrives at a party and introduces himself to the first person he sees and asks, "What is your IQ?"

The man responds, "It's 241."

"That is wonderful!" says Albert. "We will talk about the Grand Unification Theory and the mysteries of the Universe. We will have much to discuss!"

Next Albert introduces himself to a woman and asks, "What is your IQ?"

The lady answers, "It's 144."

"That is great!" responds Albert. "We can discuss politics and current affairs. We will have much to discuss!"

Albert goes to another person and asks, "What is your IQ?"

The man says, "It's 51."

Albert responds, "How about them Maple Leafs?"

Tough Night

Sidney Crosby walks into the Pittsburgh changing room to find his teammates looking glum.

"What's up?" he asks.

They reply, "We're having trouble getting motivated for this game—it's only Washington."

Crosby says, "I think I can beat them by myself—you guys go to the bar and relax." So Crosby goes and plays Washington by himself while his teammates head off to the nearest bar.

Q: How do you know the lockout is over?

A: The Panthers are already out of the playoffs.

After a few drinks, the rest of the team wonders how the game is going, so they ask the bartender to turn on the TV. The score reads: "Pittsburgh 1, Washington 0 (Crosby, 10th min, 1st period)." After several more drinks, they check the final score on the TV. It says, "Pittsburgh 1, Washington 1 (Finger, 19th min, 3rd period)."

They can't believe that Crosby has single-handedly pulled a draw against Washington, so they rush to the stadium to congratulate him. However, he is sitting with his head in his hands.

"I've let you down," he wails.

"Don't be silly," they say. "You got a draw against Washington—and they only scored at the very end."

"No, you don't understand!" he cries "I have, I've let you down! Stupid, stupid, stupid! I got sent off after 12 minutes!"

Three Wishes

A man is strolling along the riverside in Chicago when he spots a bottle floating in the water. The bottle drifts ashore. When he picks up the bottle and opens it, out pops a Genie.

"Master, you have released me from my bondage in this bottle. Ask any three wishes, and I will grant them to you."

The man thinks for a moment and says, "I would like the following three things to happen this year—the Toronto Blue Jays win the World Series, the Toronto Raptors win the NBA title and Toronto Maple Leafs win the Stanley Cup."

The Toronto Maple Leafs—green in October, brown in November and blown away in December.

OUR FAVOURITE TEAMS   103

The Genie thinks about this for a moment and jumps back into the bottle.

Look What I Found

Three hockey fans are on their way to a game when one notices a foot sticking out of the bushes by the side of the road. They stop and discover a nude female, drunk and passed out.

Out of respect for the lady, the Boston Bruins fan takes off his cap and places it over her right breast. The New York Rangers fan takes off his cap and places it over her left breast. Following their lead, the New Jersey Devils fan takes off his cap and places it over her crotch.

Q: What does a Jets fan do after his team wins the Cup?

A: He turns off the Playstation.

The police are then called, and when the officer arrives, he conducts his inspection. First, he lifts up the Bruins cap, replaces it and writes down some notes. Next, he lifts the Rangers cap, replaces it and writes down some more notes.

The officer then lifts the Devils cap, replaces it, lifts it again and replaces it. He ponders for a while, then lifts it one more time and replaces it.

Meanwhile, the Devils fan is getting upset and finally asks, "What are you, a pervert or something? Why do you keep lifting and looking, lifting and looking?"

"Well," says the officer, "I'm a little confused. Normally, when I look under a Devils hat, I find an *sshole."

Mortal Combat

A Senators fan and a Leafs fan get into a car accident. Both cars are totally demolished, but, amazingly, nobody is hurt. The Senators fan's car has a Senators sticker clearly visible, and the Leafs fan's car has a Leafs sticker clearly visible. After they crawl out of their cars, the Leafs fan says, "So, you're a Senators fan. That's interesting. I'm a Leafs fan. Wow! Just look at our cars. There's nothing left, but fortunately, we are unhurt. This must be a sign from God that we should meet and be friends and live together in peace the rest of our days."

The Senators fan replies "I agree with you completely—this must be a sign from God! And look at this! Here's another miracle. My car is completely demolished, but this bottle of whiskey didn't break. Surely God wants us to drink this and celebrate our good fortune."

Q: How many Habs fans does it take to screw in a lightbulb?

A: 12...one to screw in the bulb and 11 to talk about how great the old bulb was.

He hands the bottle to the Leafs fan. The Leafs fan nods his head in agreement, opens the bottle and takes a few big swigs, then hands it back to the Senators fan. The Senators fan takes the bottle, puts the cap back on and hands it back to the Leafs fan.

The Leafs fan asks, "Aren't you having any?"

The Senators fan replies, "No, I think I'll just wait for the police."

News Flash: This just in! NHL lockout now in effect. Edmonton Oilers fans are disappointed by the possibility of not being disappointed again this year.

Trust Issues

There is a huge fire at the All-Star game. Three hockey fans wearing the jerseys of their favorite teams are stranded on the roof: a Montreal fan, a Boston fan and a Detroit fan. The fire department comes with a blanket and yells to the Canadiens fan to jump. When he jumps, the firefighters move the blanket to the right, and the man hits the sidewalk with a splat.

The firefighters then call to the Boston fan to jump. He refuses. The would-be rescuers explain that they didn't catch the first man because they hate the Canadiens. The fan, who also hates the Canadiens, decided to trust the firefighters and jumps. Again, they move the blanket to the right, and the fan hits the ground with a splat.

Finally, they call to the Detroit Red Wings fan to jump. He also refuses. The firefighters explain that they really hated the Bruins, but the Red Wings fan isn't swayed.

He says, "I don't trust you. Lay the blanket down, and then I'll jump!"

What Kind of Fan are You?

A kindergarten teacher tells her class she's a big Devils fan. She's really excited about it and asks the kids if they're Devils fans too. Everyone wants to impress the teacher and say they are too, except one kid named Dougie.

Q: What time is it in Montreal?

A: Twelve past Carey Price.

The teacher looks at Dougie and says, "Doug, you're not a Devils fan?"

He says, "Nope, I'm a Rangers fan!"

She says, "Well why are you a Rangers fan and not a Devils fan?"

Dougie replies, "Well, my mom is a Rangers fan, and my dad is a Rangers fan, so I'm a Rangers fan."

The teacher's not very happy. In fact, she's a little hot under the collar.

She says, "Well, if your mom's an idiot, and your dad's a moron, then what would you be?"

Dougie replies, "Then I'd be a Devils fan!"

Politically Correct

Bowing to political correctness and pressure from the Native American community, the Chicago

Blackhawks have changed their name. They will now be known as the Chicago Tampons—a name chosen because the team is good for only one period and doesn't have a second line.

First guy: "Did you hear Gary Bettman attended his first Montreal Canadiens home game?"

Second guy: "No, what about it?"

First guy: "He thought the letters CH at center ice in the Bell Centre stood for 'Center Hice.'"

In Hell

One day, Satan is out for a walk through hell, making sure things are running smoothly. When he gets to the Lake of Fire, he sees a man sitting by the lake, relaxing in a lawn chair and not sweating or looking uncomfortable at all.

Perplexed, Satan approaches the man and asks, "Young man, are you not hot or bothered by this heat?"

The man replies, "Oh no, not at all. I lived in downtown Ottawa, and this weather is just like a typical July day in the city."

Q: What will be the distinctive feature of the Dallas Stars new arena?

A: The seats will be placed with their backs to the ice.

Satan does not think this is a good sign, so he rushes back to his office and turns up the heat in hell another 100 degrees. Satisfied with himself, he again returns to the Lake of Fire to check on the young man.

When the devil gets there, the man is showing a few beads of sweat, but that is all.

Again, Satan asks the Ottawa native, "Are you not hot and uncomfortable yet?"

The young man looks up and says, "No, the temperature is just like a hot August day in Ottawa. I'm coping with it just fine."

Satan decides that he has to do something drastic to make this man's stay in hell unpleasant. He goes back to his office, turns the heat all the way down and then turns up the air conditioning. The temperature in hell quickly drops well below zero. He goes to check on the young man, and as he approaches the Lake of Fire, he notices that it is now frozen over. He also sees the young man jumping up and down, wildly waving his arms and yelling into the air.

> *Q: What do a fine wine and the Minnesota Wild have in common?*
>
> *A: They both spend a lot of time in the cellar, cost too much and are only enjoyed on select occasions.*

This looks promising! thinks Satan. Coming closer, he finally makes out what the man is shouting.

"The Senators have won the Stanley Cup! The Senators have won the Stanley Cup!"

Chapter 6
To Err is Hockey Player

While it is easy to make fun of the owners and Gary Bettman during the lockouts, the players are not perfect either. We place these guys on pedestals, but once you look a little deeper, you can see that they are just normal guys who make stupid choices and say stupid things. Over the last three lockouts, the players have provided quite a few examples of strange, weird and stupid behavior both on and off the ice. Here are just a few humorous examples.

Police Report

A guy gets mugged. He notices that the mugger has bad teeth and figures he must be either an out-of-work, locked-out hockey player or British.

Note to Players: Mullets aren't cool. Sorry, bro, the party in the back has been postponed. Now that the lockout is in effect and you don't have the helmet to hide that hideous haircut, its time to join the 21st century and kill that thing attached to your head.

Note to Goaltenders: Wearing a hockey mask now means you're a murderer. I know, I know, but Jason Voorhees ruined it for everyone. You might think you're sporting the latest, greatest in hockey tech, but the kids at your child's sleep away camp are running away from you screaming, not cheering.

Wrath of God

Tampa Bay Lightning forward Martin St. Louis is playing in a charity hockey game in the parking lot of a church when he takes a shot on net, missing widely. "Damn it, I missed!" he shouts.

"You shouldn't say that," says the church priest.

"Why not?" asks St. Louis. "Will I be struck by a bolt of lightning or something?"

"Yes, you might well be," says the priest.

A moment later there is a terrific flash and a bolt of lightning shoots down from the sky. It narrowly avoids St. Louis but strikes the priest dead. And suddenly a voice from above booms: "Damn it, I missed!"

A huge NHL rookie is at his first training camp with the Buffalo Sabres.

"Can you check?" asks the coach.

"Watch this," says the rookie, who skates straight into the boards and knocks out the glass.

"Wow!" says the coach. "But can you skate fast?"

TO ERR IS HOCKEY PLAYER

111

"Of course I can skate fast," says the rookie. He's off like a shot and skates the length of the rink twice in less than 10 seconds.

"Great," says the coach. "But can you pass the puck?"

The rookie then rolls his eyes and hesitates for a moment. "Well sir," he replies, "if I can swallow it, I can probably pass it."

Wrath of Satan

To the horror of the locals of Nashville, Satan suddenly appears in the main street of town one Sunday morning. Everyone rushes indoors except for Nashville Predator Mike Fisher, who calmly stays on the park bench reading his book. Satan is furious that this one person should not be afraid.

> Happiness for a hockey player is seeing Gary Bettman on the side of a milk carton.

"Aren't you scared of me, tiny human?" screams Satan through his fanged teeth.

"Nope," says Mike Fisher.

"Aren't you terrified that I am going to wreak havoc in your community and take away everything you own?"

"Nope."

By now steam is coming out of Satan's ears. He rages, "You do know who I am, don't you?"

"Sure do. Been playing in your brother Gary Bettman's league for years now."

NHLPA Dues

Forget the slander you have heard,
Forget the hasty unkind word.
Forget the quarrel and the cause,
Forget the whole affair, because
Forgetting is the only way.
Forget the trials you have had,
Forget the weather if it's bad,
Forget the knocker, he's a freak,
Forget him seven days a week.
Forget the gray lines in your hair.
Forget you're not a billionaire,
Forget the coffee when it's cold,
Forget to knock, forget to scold,
Forget to even get the blues,
BUT DON'T FORGET TO PAY YOUR DUES!

A dedicated NHLPA member is in Las Vegas and decides to check out the local brothels. When he gets to the first one, he asks the madam, "Is this a union house?"

"No, I'm sorry, it isn't," she says.

"Well, if I pay you $100, what cut do the girls get?" he asks.

World's Shortest Book: *What Do We Want? Money! When Do We Want It? NOW!* by the NHLPA

"The house gets $80 and the girl gets $20."

Mightily offended at such unfair dealings, the man stomps off down the street in search of a more equitable shop. His search continues until he finally reaches a brothel where the madam says, "Why yes, this is a union house."

"And if I pay you $100, what cut do the girls get?" he questions.

"The girls get $80 and the house gets $20."

"That's more like it!" the NHLPA member says. He looks around the room, points to a stunningly attractive redhead, plunks down his $100 and says, "I'd like her for the night."

"I'm sure you would, sir," says the madam, as she scoops up his money and gestures to a grotesque woman in her seventies, "but Ethel here has seniority."

In a Bar

Sidney Crosby and Colby Armstrong accidentally walk into a gay bar while killing time during the lockout. As they sit down, a man walks up to Sidney and asks him to dance.

Embarrassed, he turns to Armstrong and whispers, "Help me out of this!"

So Armstrong grabs the guy, slams him up against the wall and mumbles something menacingly into his face. Once out of Armstrong's clutches, the guy apologizes and hurries away.

"Wow," Sidney says. "Thanks! What did you say to him?"

Armstrong shrugs and replies, "Told him we're on our honeymoon."

Down and Out

A Canadian hockey player is playing hockey in Europe during the lockout. Down on his luck, he robs a bank. When the police arrive, they chase after him. He runs into a corner, and the police are unable to catch him…because Europeans don't go into corners.

Sidney Crosby and Evgeni Malkin are out in the woods hunting when Crosby collapses. He doesn't seem to be breathing and his eyes are glazed.

Malkin takes out his phone and calls the emergency services. He gasps, "I think my friend is dead! What can I do?"

The operator says, "Calm down, I can help. First, let's make sure he's dead."

There is silence, then a gunshot. Back on the phone, Malkin says: "Okay, now what?

Honey!

A player who's had one too many concussions returns early from a stint playing hockey in a European league and goes home to find his wife in bed with another man.

"What the hell are you doing?" he screams as he drops his bags.

Unfazed, his wife turns to her lover and says, as she rolls her eyes, "See…I told you he was stupid."

Bobby Orr walks into an ice cream parlor. With some discomfort, he slides onto a stool and orders a banana spit.

The waitress asks, "Crushed nuts?"

He replies, "No, bad knees."

Forgive Me for I Have Sinned

A great hockey player is killed tragically, and, arriving at heaven's gates, he comes face to face with the angel on duty.

"Is there any reason why you shouldn't be allowed to enter the kingdom of heaven?" asks the angel.

"Well," says the hockey player, "there was one time when I cheated in the Stanley Cup playoffs."

"I see," says the angel. "Tell me about it."

"Well," says the hockey player. "I was playing for the Montreal Canadiens against the Toronto Maple Leafs, and I used my skate to kick in a goal. The referee didn't see it, and it counted."

"And what was the final score?" asks the angel.

"That was the only goal," says the hockey player. "We won 1–0 and took the Cup back to Montreal."

"Well, that's not too serious. I think we can let you in," says the angel.

"Oh, *merveilleux*!" exclaims the hockey player. "It's been on my mind for years. Thanks a lot, St. Peter."

"That's okay," says the angel, ushering the hockey player in. "And by the way, it's St. Peter's day off today. I'm St. Jean Baptiste."

Top 10 Ways the Los Angeles Kings Spent Their Time Off After Winning the Stanley Cup

10. Joyriding on the Zamboni.

9. Skeet shooting on the White House lawn.

8. Watching *Ellen*.

7. Practicing for the role of that adorable skating bunny in the Ice Capades.

6. Watching recordings of the 2012 playoffs 7000 times.

5. Crank calling Alexander Ovechkin.

4. Playing golf with the Toronto Maple Leafs.

3. Eating.

2. Keeping their sticks waxed, if you know what I mean.

1. Doing Stanley Cup-sized Jello shots.

Before the lockout ended, the NHL considered replacing the men with women but decided not to because they have to change their pads after every period.

Lockout Golf

Out golfing with the Toronto Maple Leafs after another year of missing the playoffs, the team's physical therapist tees off on the golf course. She slices her shot and hits one of the players standing on the adjacent green. The player collapses in agony with his hand pressed firmly between his legs. The physical therapist runs over and says, "Don't worry, I have medical training. I can help reduce the pain."

The player lets her go to work, and she opens his pants and massages his privates. After a minute of vigorous rubbing, she says, "Does that feel better?"

The player replies, "Yes, thank you. But I think you broke my thumb."

Hockey players have been complaining about the inequities of the CBA for a long time, but with no teeth no one could understand them.

Top 10 Reasons Not to Date a Hockey Player

10. They're always hugging each other.

9. They don't know how not to play rough.

8. Their sticks break.

7. They can't get wood.

6. They often miss the target.

5. They can't always find the opening.

4. They work in 45-second shifts.

3. They always want to do it on the ice.

2. When they make a nice move, they want to see the slow-motion replay.

1. Their protection doesn't always work.

News Flash: This just in! There has been a terrible tragedy down at the local hockey pond where the Newfoundland NHLers have been practicing during the lockout. The players all drowned during spring training."

Priorities

A little known fact: the first testicular guard "cup" was used in hockey in 1874, but the first helmet wasn't used until 1974. In other words, it took 100 years for players to realize that their brains were also important.

Across the Pond

Sidney Crosby has had enough of the NHL lockout so he decides to go over to Europe to play in the Swiss League. Just before a face-off, Mark Streit lines up next to Crosby and says, "Hey, you're a Canadian, right?"

Crosby swells out his chest and says, "Damn right I am and proud of it."

Streit smiles and quips, "Then what are you in the bathroom?"

Confused, Crosby looks at Streit and asks, "What?"

Streit laughs and responds, "European."

Two Russian hockey players board a flight out of Toronto after the announced lockout of NHL hockey. One sits in the window seat, and the other sits in the middle seat. Just before take-off, a Canadian hockey player gets on and takes the aisle seat. After take-off, the Canadian kicks off his shoes, wiggles his toes and is settling in when the Russian in the window seat says, "I think I'll get up and get a beer."

"No problem," says the Canadian. "I'll get it for you. I, like you, am off to play hockey in Russia."

While he is gone, one of the Russians picks up the Canadian's shoe and spits in it. When the Canadian returns with the beer, the other Russian

says, "That looks good. I think I'll have one, too."
Again, the Canadian obligingly goes to fetch a beer,
and while he is gone, the other Russian picks up
the other shoe and spits in it. When the Canadian returns to his seat, the men all sit back and enjoy the flight. As the plane is landing, the Canadian slips his feet into his shoes and knows immediately what has happened.

> Usually [it's] give me your money or I'm going to hurt you. Not give me your money AND I'm going to hurt you.
>
> –Phoenix Coyotes forward Shane Doan

"Why does it have to be this way?" he asks. "How long must this go on? This fighting between our nations, this hatred, this animosity? This spitting in shoes and pissing in beers?"

Help, Fire!

Roberto Luongo is walking along the street one day when he hears screams from a nearby building. He looks up to see smoke billowing from a fourth-floor window and a woman leaning out, holding a baby.

"Help! Help!" screams the woman. "I need someone to catch my baby!"

A crowd of onlookers has gathered, but no one is confident enough to catch a delicate little baby from such a great height. Then Luongo steps forward.

"I'm a professional goaltender," he yells to the woman. "I'm well known for my quick hands. Drop the baby, and I will catch it. Lady, I catch frozen pucks traveling at speeds over 60 miles per hour."

"Okay, then," says the woman. "When I drop my baby, treat it as if you were catching a puck."

On the count of three, the woman drops the baby. Everyone holds their breath as Luongo steadies himself to catch the falling baby. They watch as Luongo stretches out his hands only to see the baby go right through. "Damn," he says. "I thought I had that one."

(Don't worry, the baby lands on a pile of pillows and is saved, completely unharmed but like everyone else, disappointed in Luongo.)

On a Date

An NHL enforcer's girlfriend persuades him to take her to a restaurant, but he isn't used to eating out with her and doesn't know what to order from the menu.

"Why don't you have what I choose?" she suggests.

"What? I couldn't do that and leave you hungry."

Hockey players are noted for their sex drives, and because of the lockout, the players' wives are being run ragged with all the sex. One wife pushes her horny husband away.

"Sorry, honey," she says, "but I have a gynecologist appointment in the morning and I want to stay fresh."

Undeterred, he pushes up against her. "Do you have a dental appointment?"

Vegas High Jinx

Evander Kane flies to Vegas for the weekend to gamble. He looses the shirt off his back and has nothing left but a quarter and the second half of his round-trip ticket. If he can just get to the airport he'll be able to get home. So he goes out to the front of the casino where a cab is waiting.

He gets in and explains his situation to the cabbie. He promises to send the driver money from home, even offering his credit card numbers, driver's license number, address and so forth, but to no avail. The cabbie yells, "If you don't have $15, get the hell out of my cab!" So Evander has to hitchhike to the airport and is barely in time to catch his flight.

One year later, Kane, having worked hard to regain his financial success when hockey returned from lockout, returns to Vegas, and this time he wins big. Feeling pretty good about himself, he goes out to the front of the casino to catch a ride back to the airport.

Naturally, sitting at the end of a long line of cabs is his old buddy who had refused to give him a ride when he was down on his luck. Kane thinks for a moment about how he can make the driver pay for his lack of charity, and he comes up with the perfect plan.

He gets in the first cab in line. "How much for a ride to the airport?" he asks.

"Fifteen bucks," comes the reply.

"And how much for you to give me a blowjob on the way?"

"What? Get the hell out of my cab!"

Kane gets into the back of each cab in the long line and asks the same questions, with the same result.

When he finally gets to his old friend at the back of the line, he climbs in and asks "How much for a ride to the airport?"

The cabbie replies, "Fifteen bucks."

Kane says, "Okay," and off they go. Then, as they drive slowly past the long line of cabs, Kane gives a big smile and thumbs-up sign to each driver.

Did you see Alex Semin's last fight? I hear he picked the guy up and started playing him like a guitar!

Top 10 Pickup Lines of Locked-out Players Looking for Love

10. "So, this guy says he hates hockey players because they have no tact and are easily distracted. So I—Hey! Babe! Wanna do the nasty?"

9. "You heard right: I only take off this mask for two things."

8. "I may be toothless, sweaty and all black and blue, but I make a mean quiche."

7. "Me take you to eat."

6. "Would you like a Zamboni ride?"

5. "I'm Lanny MacDonald, and this mustache doesn't ride itself."

4. "C'mon baby, the iceman cometh...but never too soon."

3. "Well if I can't score, can I get an assist?"

2. "You know, less teeth means more tongue."

1. "You want to check my stick curvature?"

How Some Players Spent Their Time Off

Ilya Bryzgalov

Anyone who has ever played hockey will tell you that goaltenders are a weird bunch. They stay at one end of the ice, shielded by layers of padding, caged in behind fiberglass and steel, alone in their crease, standing in front of speeding frozen pucks. In the history of the NHL, there have been some weird goaltenders. Take for example Patrick

Roy—Hall of Fame goaltender for the Montreal Canadiens and the Colorado Avalanche. Roy was a goalie filled with little quirks. Every game he would constantly talk to his goal posts, even thanking them when a puck would career off them. Another Montreal Canadiens goaltender, Jacques Plante, would sit and knit in the locker room before, during and after games to relax. The odd goaltender tradition has been carried on today by Ilya Bryzgalov.

The Russian goaltender and member of the Philadelphia Flyers (at the time of writing) has always been a favorite of the fans and especially the sound bite–hungry media. After one particularly bad game in which he lost 9–8 to the Winnipeg Jets, Bryzgalov told the media that he "stunk" and that he probably could not stop a ball, let alone a puck. He is also well known by his teammates as a dreamer, and the thing that most often makes him pause is pondering the universe. Once asked by a reporter what would he do in life if he was not a goaltender, Bryzgalov didn't pause for even a second before saying, "Astronaut!"

The reporter, John Gonzalez of Comcast Sportsnet Philly, followed up the astronaut angle by getting into a rather strange discussion with the Flyers goaltender. Gonzalez wrote, "Bryzgalov began a long dissertation about the American space program versus the Soviet/Russian space program and which was superior. He noted that the first two animals in space were Russian dogs, which led to a strange exchange between Bryzgalov and a reporter about who had lost more monkeys in space—the Americans or the Soviets/Russians. Bryzgalov conceded that too many monkeys had lost their lives in that vocation."

'The problem with monkeys," Bryzgalov quipped, "they push the wrong buttons.'"

In an HBO documentary on hockey called *24/7*, in which a film crew follows around two NHL teams, Bryzgalov was more than happy to continue talking about his obsession with space.

"I'm very into the universe, you know like how it was created, you know, like, what is it, you know? [The] solar system is so humongous big, right? But if you see like our solar system and our galaxy on the side, you know, like, we're so small you can never see it. Our galaxy is like huge, but if you see the big picture our galaxy [is] like a small tiny-like dot in the universe."

During the 2011–12 lockout, instead of playing in the Russian Kontinental Hockey League (KHL) or taking some time off to be with his family, Bryzgalov spent his time in Russia furthering his obsession with space and being an astronaut. He visited the Yuri Gagarin Cosmonaut Training Center just outside Moscow in what locals call Star City and participated in the facility's full cosmonaut training program, which included the infamous g-force test, where they spin the trainee in an incredibly large centrifuge until the person passes out from the g-forces. For Bryzgalov, though, training to get into space might not be enough, and had the lockout gone on for a full season, he might have taken the great leap into the beyond in his quest to solve the greatest mysteries of the universe.

Johnny Oduya

While many NHLers left to play hockey in European leagues and a few in the North American pro leagues, Johnny Oduya made a promise to himself that if the 2012–13 lockout went anywhere past the beginning of October he would take a trip with a few of his friends to Thailand to celebrate one of their birthdays. It was supposed to be nothing more than a relaxing vacation, a getaway from all the negativity that was surrounding the players and the management as they battled it out in the boardroom. Hockey was supposed to be the last thing on Oduya's mind as he packed his swim trunks and suntan lotion, but hockey never leaves a hockey player's mind. A quick check on the Internet and Oduya found a hockey team called the Flying Farangs, who just so happened to be playing in a charity tournament called the Land of Smiles Ice Hockey Classic.

> I wonder if the owners of Boston, New York, Washington etc, etc, have endured any of the injuries that I or any other player in the NHL [has] endured. Still they probably sit there smoking the same brand of cigar, sipping the same cognac, and going on vacation to one of five houses they own...While we sit here knowing they want to take 20 percent of our paychecks. One half to three quarters of my peers will have to work for the next 50 years of their lives....
>
> –New Jersey Devils Forward Krys Barch via Twitter

> All hockey players are bilingual. They know English and profanity.
>
> –Gordie Howe

Apparently this tournament had welcomed NHLers in the past, including Troy Crowder and Neal Broten, so Oduya figured he might as well stay in game shape while on vacation.

The tournament featured up to 60 men's league teams from around the world in a championship tournament whose proceeds go to charity.

After contacting the tournament organizers, who instantly agreed to have Oduya in their tournament, he spent a few days getting accustomed to playing with his new teammates and then started the tourney. In a strange twist, former Toronto Maple Leafs goaltender Vesa Toskala played as a forward in the tournament for the Finnish team.

With a current NHLer on the team, the Flying Farangs of Bangkok easily won their first ever Land of Smiles tournament championship, defeating a team from Abu Dhabi in the final. After a few more days on the beach, Oduya flew back to his native Sweden to spend time with family and train in a more usual setting.

Sidney Crosby

It is a night just like any other down at a local Pittsburgh floor hockey rink. The guys gather before the game, strap on their equipment, chat idly about their lives and hit the floor for their weekly game. As anyone who ever played hockey knows, sometimes it is not easy to find a goaltender. So when one of the regulars said he would be bringing a friend in to replace a missing goaltender, no one questioned it, and the game went on as normal.

Little did they know that the regular player's friend just happened to be the biggest star in hockey, Sidney Crosby.

"My buddy plays in the league there. I talked to him about playing," Crosby said. "I played a lot of goalie in street hockey growing up and stuff. Just asked if he needed a goalie. He said sure, and I came out. It was cool."

Desperate for some sort of hockey to play, Sidney thought it would be fun to surprise a few fans and get in a good workout at the same time. The most amazing part is that no one realized who was in goal for the majority of the game; not his own teammates or the opposing team taking shots at the most famous person in hockey today. The only person to clue into the surprise was the referee, who shouted, "Holy cow! That's Sidney Crosby!"

> It seems like for [the NHL], it's become the bully in the playground. It's like, "We think we can take your cookies, too."
>
> –Calgary Flames forward Mike Cammalleri

For the record, Crosby shutout the opposing team in a 4–0 win. The name of Sidney's ball hockey team, no joke, was Flyers Suck.

Evander Kane's Twitter No-No

This most recent NHL lockout particularly disappointed hockey's fan base. Things just did not seem to add up for the fans. Since the last lockout, most of the franchises in the league were making millions of dollars, players' salaries had increased to ridiculous levels, and forget about job security issues when players were signing remarkable contracts, such as Ilya Kovalchuk whose 15-year deal would see him making millions into his mid-forties.

It was hard for the average Joe fan to see why the lockout occurred in the first place. Just a bunch of greedy rich kids crying over a few percentage points. This disconnect grew as the lockout stretched beyond the preseason and well into the first 20 or so games, and the lack of hockey began to affect businesses that rely on the sport to stay afloat. Restaurants were not hiring, bars sat empty and sports stores were forced to close. The anger among fans this time around was getting louder and more nasty as time went on. So it is hard to fathom why Evander Kane of the Winnipeg Jets did what he did on Twitter.

With no end in sight to the lockout, Evander Kane and some friends decided to

> I prefer the NHL style of hockey. You always think European hockey is going to be more wide open and with more scoring and that sort of stuff, but it's almost the opposite. There is less scoring...There was a lot more grabbing, holding and clutching than I expected. Because of the big ice, there's a lot of man-on-man play. In the playoffs, they were just draped all over me, and nothing got called. They let everything go. I remember forward looking at me and not even looking at the play, with their stick between my legs.
>
> –Dan Boyle, Tampa Bay Lightning defenseman, on his season spent in Sweden during the 2004–05 lockout

go to Vegas to get their minds off hockey. The young hockey star seemed to have a good time in Sin City because just shortly after arriving, he tweeted a picture of himself on the balcony of one of the fancy hotels overlooking the infamous strip holding one large wad of cash in one hand and another wad held up to his ear with the following line: "Hey @floydmayweather pick up your phone cause I'm callin #imdifferent."

Now while it is really is no one's business what Kane does with his money or how he flaunts it, the image of Kane rubbing wads of cash all over his body posted on Twitter really got some people up in arms. With no hockey to talk about, sports radio stations, specifically radio stations in Winnipeg, were flooded with calls by angry hockey fans calling for his head. More than anything, it was the hypocrisy of players demanding more money while Kane flaunted his bills in such a public manner. For his part, Kane did not see the picture as that big of a deal, but he apologized anyway.

Blackface

Twitter is a great tool. It enables people to connect and spread information to a wide variety of people all over the globe. It can be a great thing, but it can also have a downside, as we have already seen in the case of Evander Kane. This next case, though, is on a whole new level of bad.

Hockey players, like everyone else, love Halloween. They love the chance to dress up and be someone other than themselves for a night of innocent fun. Most hockey players are professional people, and though they relish the opportunity to take off their skates and have a little fun, most realize that they are still public figures and are under a different level of scrutiny. Tyler Bozak of the Toronto Maple Leafs found this fact out the hard way when he posted a picture of himself in costume for Halloween. The problem was that Bozak, a white male, painted his face black to look like Michael Jackson of the Thriller era.

Now though Bozak never made any racist remarks and called the costume a tribute to one of his musical idols, painting your face black comes with a lot of nasty historical baggage.

The practice of painting your face black, or blackface, dates back to the 19th century, when Vaudeville actors performed stereotypical caricatures of black people for a paying audience. The characters would usually dance about on stage in a funny manner wearing wigs and tattered clothing, generally making fools of themselves. These characters came to symbolize and reinforce the racist attitudes of white America. Many people over the years have gotten themselves in trouble for painting their faces black, including a few hockey players like Adam Burish and Patrick Kane of the Chicago Blackhawks, who showed up to a 2009 Halloween party dressed as Dennis Rodman and Scottie Pippen, and Raffi Torres of the Phoenix Coyotes and his wife, who painted their faces black and showed up to a party as Jay-Z and Beyonce.

While not overtly racist, the costume is racially insensitive and thoughtless. The worst part about the situation is that Bozak had already dressed in blackface before, appearing at an earlier Halloween party as a Jamaican bobsledder.

Flyers Go Hollywood

When hockey players in the past have made the jump to the silver screen or to television, the results have not always been, well, for lack of a better word, good. Anyone remember Wayne Gretzky hosting Saturday Night Live (if you can find the Honolulu Hockey skit, you will see) or Alexandre Daigle's short acting career? Yet despite the mounting evidence that hockey players should stick to the ice, every now and again Hollywood comes knocking. The most recent example is that of director Judd Apetow's latest adult comedic offering *This is Forty,* starring Paul Rudd and Leslie Mann.

> Gary Bettman's autobiograhy is in stores now. It's titled "How to destroy a sport and a nation."
>
> –Montreal Canadiens forward Brandon Prust

In the script, the character played by Leslie Mann goes to a bar with her friends for a girls' night out, and they just happen to meet some hockey players in the bar. The script called for the stereotypical toothless hockey player, and a member of the Philadelphia Flyers somehow got wind of this. He recommended Ian Lapierriere for the role because just that season Lapierriere had lost seven of his teeth after getting hit in the face with a puck, twice. Well, with a lockout looming, Lapierriere naturally jumped at the chance to be in a Hollywood movie, and he also managed to get a few of his teammates added to the movie. Scott Hartnell, Matt Carle and James van Riemsdyk joined Lapierriere. Hartnell got to exclaim proudly in the movie, "We play for the Philadelphia Flyers."

But hands down the best part of the scene happens when sultry starlet Megan Fox asks the players if they have all their teeth, to which Laperriere responds, "Well, I have all my teeth, except these ones." He then removes his false teeth and hands them to Fox and asks her to try them on. During a press conference for the film, Laperriere was asked how it felt to see Megan Fox wearing his teeth. "Not too many guys get to say that," he crowed.

"You're the only guy in the world to have his teeth in her mouth," Judd Apatow added. After a few more lines by Carle and Riemsdyk, the scene ends, as does the acting careers of the hockey players. Fans of proper cinema breathed a sigh of relief when hockey returned in 2013 to ensure that no other hockey players make anymore cameos in movies. For now!

Visit

Sidney Crosby has plenty of time on his hands during the lockout, so one day he decides to do a benefit appearance at a senior citizens home in Pittsburgh. He goes up to one of the elderly ladies, sits down beside her and says, "Do you know who I am?"

She replies, "No, but go to the front desk. They'll tell you who you are."

The Sharks picked up Scott Gomez off waivers. They were drawn to him because he was bleeding and looked like an injured seal.

Car Loan

Before leaving for Russia to play hockey in the KHL, Ilya Kovalchuk drives his Ferrari to a downtown New York City bank and goes in to ask for an immediate loan of $5000. The loan officer, taken aback, requests collateral.

"Well, here are the keys to my Ferrari," says Kovalchuk.

> Knock, knock!
> Who's there?
> Sak!
> Sak who?
> KOIVU!!!

The loan officer has the car driven into the bank's underground parking lot for safe keeping and gives Kovalchuk the $5000.

Two months later, Kovalchuk walks through the bank's doors and asks the loan officer to settle up his loan and get the car back. "That will be $5000 in principal and $47.50 in interest," says the loan officer.

Kovalchuk writes out and check, takes his keys and starts to walk away. "Wait sir," says the loan officer. "While you were gone, I found out you were a mutli-million dollar hockey player. Why in the world would you need to borrow $5000?"

Kovalchuk smiles. "Where else could I park my Ferrari in Manhattan for two months and pay only $47.50?"

Same Old Tricks

Dany Heatley takes his hot date out in his new sports car. A few miles down the road, he turns to her and says, "If I do 200 miles per hour, will you take your clothes off?"

She says it sounds like fun, so he steps on the gas. When the speedometer touches the 200 mark, she begins to strip. Distracted by her state of undress, he takes his eyes off the road for a second and crashes into a pole. The girl is thrown clear without a scratch but all her clothes are still trapped in the car, along with Heatley.

"Go and get help," he shouts.

"I can't," she says. "I'm stark naked, and I don't want anyone to see me."

He points to one of his shoes that was thrown clear. "Cover your crotch with that, and go and get help. Please!"

> The hockey lockout has been settled. They have stopped bickering...and can now get down to some serious bloodshed.
>
> –Conan O'Brien

So she picks up the shoe, covers herself with it and runs 2 miles to the nearest gas station.

"Help! Help!" she yells to the elderly attendant. "My boyfriend's stuck!"

The attendant glances down at the shoe covering her crotch and says, "I'm sorry, miss, he's too far in."

Money Talks

Alexander Ovechkin walks into a bank and says to the female teller at the window, "I want to open a bloody account."

"I beg your pardon," says the teller. "What did you say?"

"Listen, damn you," snarls Ovechkin. "I said I want to open a bloody account—right now!"

"I'm sorry, sir," says the teller, "but I am afraid we do not tolerate that kind of language in this bank." And with that, she leaves the window and reports the customer's behavior to the manager. The manager walks over to confront him.

"Now what seems to be the problem?" asks the manager.

"There's no problem," says Ovechkin. "I just signed a hundred million dollar contract, and I want to open a bloody account in the damn bank!"

"I see," says the manager, "and this bitch is giving you a hard time?"

Why Hockey is the Best Fighting Sport

- It's like a street fight, but it's organized into teams and takes place on skates.

- It's okay to punch, hit or slash other people with your stick. It's called "part of the game."

- Fans actually pay to see players fight and play a little hockey.

- Hockey violence is better than boxing, and they do it 70 games a year.

- When you get punished for fighting, you get to sit down for five minutes, and then you get to play and fight again.

- Hockey coaches actually hire players who do not score, but instead beat up people.

- You won't get in trouble with your boss when you slug opposing players, and there may even be a bounty.

Bryz in Space

Ilya Bryzgalov, goaltender for the Philadelphia Flyers, is well known for his love of space. Well, long after retiring, he finally realizes his dream of leaving his earthly bounds when he qualifies for the Russian space mission to Mars. It is a solo mission, but Bryzgalov takes up the challenge.

Seen on a bumper sticker: Be kind to animals. Hug a hockey player.

The mission is successful and Bryzgalov lands safely on the planet, but after several months he gets really lonely. One day while out exploring, he comes across a beautiful Martian woman stirring a huge pot over a campfire.

"Hi, there," he says casually. "I am from Earth. What are you doing?"

"Making babies," she explains, looking up with a coquettish smile.

Horny after so long away from Earth women, Bryz decides to give his lady skills a shot. "That's not the way we make babies on Earth," he informs the sexy green Martian lady.

"Oh, really," she says as she looks up from her pot. "How by chance do your people do it?"

"Well, it's hard to describe," he says, "but I'd be glad to show you."

"Fine," agrees the Martian maiden, and the two make love for hours in the glow of the Martian fire. Afterward, she asks, "So where are the babies?"

"Oh, they don't show up for another nine months," says Bryzgalov.

"So why'd you stop stirring?" she replies.

⋘ CHAPTER 7 ⋙

Back to Hockey!!!

While fans are stuck in a hockey-less state, it seems as if the lockout will never end, but they all eventually do, and hockey returns life back to what hockey people consider as normal. Once again fans leave their families, players get into fights and owners rake in the money. Ahh, hockey—for the pure love of sport.

Young Hockey Player

Coming home from his peewee game, young Bobby swings open the front door excitedly. Unable to attend the game, his father immediately wants to know what happened at his son's game. "So, how did you do, son?" he asks.

"You'll never believe it," Bobby says. "I was responsible for the winning goal!"

"Really? How did you do that?" inquires his dad.

Bobby replies, "I scored in my own net."

Hockey 101

A coach is describing the roles of each position on a hockey team to a group of six-year-olds. When it comes to the goalie, the coach asks, "Who knows what the goalie does?"

One bright youngster speaks up, "He takes the puck out of the net!"

Have a Happy Hockey Return

'Twas the night before Christmas and at the arena,

Nobody was working not even a cleaner.

The pucks and the sticks were stacked in a ring,

In hopes that Lord Stanley would come in the spring.

The players had scattered to places more tame,

Imagining hat tricks they'd score the next game.

The coach with his headset, the GM in his suit,

Abandoned discussions of talent and loot.

When out on the ice there arose such commotion,

It attracted a crowd, expecting some promotion.

In through the doors and down to the seats,

We gathered together with sodas and eats.

And then, like by magic they switched on the lights,

And the rink was awash with an aura quite bright.

When, what to the amazement of all should appear,

But a giant zamboni and great players in gear.

The mystical driver was macho and manly,

So we knew in an instant it must be Lord Stanley.

Quick as the wind his charges they skated,

And he whistled and shouted, yelled and berated:

"Now, Gordie! Now, Espo! Now, Dionne and Clarke!

On Gretzky! On, Dryden! On, Orr and Brad Park!

To the point with a pass, then into the slot,

Now breakaway, breakaway, get a good shot!"

As had many before them when body checks flew,

Made a pass, made a play, somehow to get through,

So back through the neutral zone, quickly they came,

Flashing skills that had brought them great fortune and fame.

And then right before us, all over the ice,

There was shooting and skating and passing quite nice.

As I turned from the rink, took a sip from my brew,

Lord S. hopped right down, joined the rest of the crew.

They were dressed in strange costumes we could tell at a glance,

With bright-colored sweaters and suspendered short pants.

New sharpened skates were laced tight on their feet,

With gloves, pads and stockings that were tidy and neat.

Their eyes, how intense! So much it was scary,

And their faces were much scarred and grizzled and hairy.

BACK TO HOCKEY!!!

Their broad crooked mouths opened wide to reveal,

The same toothless grins that had won fan appeal.

The ends of their sticks they held firmly and sure,

And their passes and shots were still sweet and pure.

Their faces and bellies were broader by far,

But they still had the fire that once made them stars.

They poked and they prodded, a few even fought,

And we smiled, contented, Old Time Hockey, we thought.

A wink from Lord S. and a smile not well hid,

Soon had us all feeling as though we were kids.

He looked on in silence, enjoying the show,

For what seemed like hours, then started to go.

And pointing a finger toward the locker room door,

And giving a shrug through the tunnel he roared.

He flipped off his skates, gave his team one last glower,

Then they all left the ice on their way to the shower.

But we heard him cry out as he stripped off his jockeys,

"Happy end of lockout to all, good night and good hockey!"

(Please read with the voice of a 14 year old girl in your head, or out loud if you wish) Okay, like next time we meet, like, we have to be nice to each other, and like totally not talk behind each other's backs, cause it upsets Gary, and Donald doesn't like it either. So everyone, just like, chill next time, okay?

Hockey in Heaven

St. Peter and Satan are having an argument one day about hockey. Satan proposes a game to be played on neutral ice between a select team from the heavenly host and his own hand-picked boys. "Very well," says the gatekeeper of heaven. "But you realize, I hope, that we've got all the good players and the best coaches."

"I know, and that's all right," Satan answers, unperturbed. "We've got all the referees."

Steven Stamkos gets off the ice during his first game back after the lockout, after taking a vicious hit. He motions to the trainer for attention and shouts that his ribs are cracked. The trainer states that he shouldn't shout things like that. "You want to appear invincible and never let the other team know where you hurt, or they will target you there."

"But my ribs are cracked!" says Stamkos.

Q: What do a hockey player and a magician have in common?

A: They both do hat tricks.

"You need to redirect it. State that you need another stick or that your skate is dull, and when I come over, tell me what you really need."

When he returns to action several weeks later, Stamkos takes a stick to the face. He keeps his head high and skates over to the bench as if nothing happened, despite the blood coming out of his eyes. He motions to the trainer and yells that there is something wrong with his skates.

The trainer asks, "What's wrong with them?"

Stamkos yells back, "I can't see out of them!"

Five guys at a hockey game:
Souvenirs: $150
Tickets: $250
Hotel and Beer: $500
Wives at home: PRICELE$$!

Now that Hockey Has Returned, Let the Cliches BEGIN!

- "Yeah, we really gave 110 percent and came out strong."
- "They were a tough team and came at us hard from the start."
- "Yeah, the goalie kept us in the game and was the reason we won."
- "We have to come out stronger in the third period and tie the game up."
- "It's about playing a full 60 minutes of hockey."

At Training Camp

A young Newfoundland-born player is drafted by the Habs and is ready to attend his first training camp.

"How will I get by?" he asks his father. "I don't speak French."

"Just speak slow," the old man says. "They understand you when you do that."

So when the young man shows up at camp, he walks up to another rookie and says, "Hi...my...name...is...John."

The other fella says, "Hi...my...name...is...Mark."

"Where...are...you...from?"

"New...found...land."

"Me...too."

"If...we're...both...from...the...Rock...then...why...are...we...wasting...our...time...speaking...French?"

After another lockout, the NHL might be creating a new contest to energize its American fans. How does it work? The first fan to actually locate a channel airing an NHL playoff game wins.

BACK TO HOCKEY!!!

Surprising Clauses in the 2012 Collective Bargaining Agreement

- The NHLPA agrees to provide a block for Gary Bettman to stand on whenever at a press conference beside Donald Fehr.
- The NHLPA assigns Mike Fisher to hold onto the association's purse.
- The NHLPA reluctantly agrees to not make fun of Gary Bettman's stature, no matter how fun it is!
- Tim Hortons is to be supplied at every meeting.
- Both sides agree to set up a fake meeting place for the next negotiations to keep Bruins owner Jeremy Jacobs out.
- NHL owners agree to leave the evil super villain Mysterio out of future negotiations.
- No one is to talk about the Phoenix Coyotes. They exist, that is all anyone needs to know.

Hockey Marriage

One man says to another: "My wife thinks I put hockey before marriage, even though we just celebrated our third season together."

"You're so involved with hockey," whines the wife, "that you can't even remember the day we were married."

"That's what you think!" counters the husband. "It was the same day I scored a hat trick."

New Rules in Post-lockout NHL

- The puck must be indiscriminate enough that it cannot be seen on television.

- Players must wear pink on their helmet, pants, jersey or skates.

- Players with a French name must wear extra pink.

- All controversial calls shall go in favor of the team that paid the referees more money.

- Coaches may only speak a maximum of five words at a time.

- No players on the ice can share the same first name unless it's Joe, Brian, Sergei or Alexander.

- Only players older than 33 may skate backward.

- The NHL must have way too many rules.

- Delay of game must always be called if the puck ends up over the glass, even if the referee threw it there.

- There must be a lockout every seven seasons.

- The best teams will all be eliminated in the first round of the playoffs.

- In 2016, the CBC must remove the batteries from the back of Don Cherry's head.

The Afghani Hockey Star

Detroit Red Wings head coach Mike Babcock sends scouts out around the world looking for a new center who will hopefully help win the Stanley Cup for Detroit. One of his scouts informs him of a young Afghani center whom he thinks will turn out to be a true superstar. So, Mike flies to Afghanistan to watch him play, is suitably impressed and arranges for him to come over to the NHL.

Two weeks later, Detroit is down 4–0 at home against Pittsburgh, with only eight minutes left. Mike gives the young Afghani center the nod to go on, and he puts him on in place of Pavel Datsyuk. The lad is a sensation. He scores five goals in eight minutes and wins the game for the Red Wings. The fans are delighted, the players and coaches are delighted and the media love the new star. When he comes off the ice, he phones his mother to tell her about his first day in the NHL.

"Hi, Mom, guess what?" he says. "I played for eight minutes today, we were down 4–0 but I scored five goals and we won. Everybody loves me. The fans, the players and the media, they all love me."

"Great," says his mother. "Let me tell you about my day. Your father got shot in the street, your sister and I were raped and beaten and your brother has joined a gang of looters, while you were having a great time."

The young lad is naturally very upset. "What can I say, Mom, I'm so sorry."

"Sorry!" says his mother. "It's your damned fault that we moved to Detroit in the first place!"

Why Hockey is Better than Sex

10. You go in 1–2 minute shifts.
9. The puck is always hard.
8. The equipment is reusable.
7. It lasts a full hour.
6. When the buzzer sounds, you're done.
5. Your parents cheer when you score.
4. A 2-on-1 or a 3-on-1 is not uncommon.
3. It is legal to play professionally.
2. You can count on it at least twice a week.
1. Periods last only 20 minutes.

Why Sex is Better than Hockey

When you get locked out of sex, there is always another team that wants you. Unless you're married—then you get locked into negotiations.

A man and his wife are sitting in the living room watching a hockey game on TV when he says to her, "Just so you know, I never want to live in a vegetative state, dependent on some machine and fluids from a bottle. If that ever happens, just pull the plug."

His wife gets up, unplugs the TV and throws out all of his beer.

Prediction

The seven dwarves are trapped in a mineshaft. Snow White runs to the entrance and yells down to them. A voice calls back from the darkness below, "The Columbus Blue Jackets will win the Stanley Cup."

Snow White sighed, "Thank God! At least Dopey is still alive."

The main difference between golf and hockey is that hockey is murder—you just want to kill the other player. Golf is suicide—you just want to kill yourself.

Canadian Sex

A woman walks into the doctor's office and complains that she is suffering from knee pain.

"Do you indulge in any activity that puts a lot of pressure on your knees?" asks the doctor.

"Well…every night, my husband and I have sex on the floor in the living room, doggy style," she shyly says.

"I see," says the doctor. "You know, there are plenty of other sexual position that you could try. Here, take this copy of the *Kama Sutra,* and you will see there are hundreds of positions to try."

She takes the book and flips through it looking at the pictures, then says to the doctor, "But there are no positions here where we can both watch the hockey game."

Moral of the Story

The children in class are asked to write a story with a moral. The next day, they read out their efforts to the class. First to go is young Jennie. She reads out loud and proud, "My daddy owns a farm and every Sunday we put the chicken eggs on the truck and drive to town to sell them at the market. But one Sunday, we hit a bump and all the eggs fell onto the road and smashed. And the moral of the story is, 'don't put all your eggs in one basket.'"

"That's very good, Jennie," says the teacher. "Now you, Ella."

Ella reads out her story: "My daddy also owns a farm. Every weekend we take the chicken eggs and put them in an incubator. Last weekend, only 8 of the 12 eggs hatched. And the moral of the story is, 'don't count your chickens before they hatch.'"

"Very nice, Ella," says the teacher. "Now let's hear from you, Johnny."

Johnny reads out his story: "My uncle was working one day in Russia when he was attacked by a huge, ugly man. My uncle took him on with his bare hands, punching his face over and over again until the big man lay on the ground. But that wasn't all. The big man had friends, and two bigger guys jumped my uncle, but he took a stick and smashed one over the head, then grabbed the other and knocked him out with one punch, breaking his front teeth."

"That's very…erm…colorful, Johnny," says the teacher, "but what is the moral of the story?"

"Don't mess with a Canadian hockey player."

A man is getting married and is standing by his bride at the church. On the ground beside him is his hockey gear.

His bride whispers, "What is your hockey crap doing here?"

The groom replies, "This is not going to take all day, is it?"

Returning Home

John Tavares returns home after playing in Europe during the lockout. Having left his beloved cat in his brother's care while he was gone, he immediately calls his brother once he lands to inquire about the cat.

"The cat is dead," his brother says bluntly.

Tavares is devastated. "You don't know how much little Wang meant to me," he sobs. "Couldn't you at least have given a little thought to a nicer way of breaking the news? Like, I don't know, maybe, 'Well, you know, the cat got out of the house one day and climbed up on the roof, and the fire department couldn't get him down and she finally died of exposure or something. Anything but, YOUR CAT IS DEAD!"

"Look, I'm really, really, really sorry," says his brother. "I will remember to change."

"Okay, forget it. How are you? How's mom?"

There was a long pause. "Uh, um. Mom's on the roof."

Game Shape

After a full off-season and 119 days of lockout, Martin Brodeur finally admits he is overweight. One morning as he is reading the newspaper, he sees a special introductory offer from a new weight-loss clinic in town. After handing over his payment, he is shown into an empty room where he is soon joined by a gorgeous blonde. "Hi," she says. "If you catch me, I'm yours."

It takes a while, but after a prolonged chase Brodeur succeeds—and is delighted to find he's lost five pounds in the process. After that experience he gives up all thoughts of dieting and manages to drop five more pounds with a brunette and eight more with a hot redhead. But he is still a few pounds overweight, and with the season fast approaching, he decides to sign up for the clinic's more drastic program.

He is waiting eagerly in an empty room when the door opens and in comes a 300-pound gay guy who grins and says, "If I catch you, you're mine."

Passion for the Game

A lady walks into a tattoo parlor. She's been told that the artist is the best. Being a huge Sidney Crosby fan, she requests that the artist put Crosby's face on her right inner thigh. After an hour of work, he finishes and shows the lady his work.

> How would you like a job where, every time you make a mistake, a big red light goes on and 18,000 people boo?
>
> –Jacques Plante

"This doesn't look anything like Crosby," she says.

So he takes out a picture of Crosby and compares them. "See, they look exactly alike."

The lady does not agree. So the artist offers to try again on the other thigh for free.

The lady comes back the next day to have her left thigh done. The artist does the tattoo and excitedly shows it to her.

"This one doesn't look like Sidney Crosby, either!" she says.

The artist insists that this one is identical to the picture of Crosby she had brought. To solve the debate, the artist calls his friend, a huge hockey fan, over to decide. The friend comes over and the lady lifts her dress to show him the tattoos.

"Hmmm, I'm not sure who the wingers are, but the center is definitely George Parros."

Intermission

A hockey fan walks into a bar in the Bell Centre during the first intermission and orders a hot dog and a beer. He downs the beer, puts the hot dog on his head, smashes it with his hand and walks out of the bar before the bartender can say a word.

During the next intermission, the hockey fan returns and once again orders a hot dog and a beer. The bartender watches in amazement as the man drinks the beer, puts the hot dog on his head, smashes it with his hand and walks out.

After the game ends, the drunk fan is back in the bar and places his order of a hot dog and a beer. But this time the bartender is waiting for him and says, "I'm sorry, we're out of hot dogs."

"Right," says the hockey fan. "I'll have a packet of chilli flavored potato chips and a beer."

He downs the beer, puts the packet of chips on his head, smashes it with his hand and heads for the door.

"Wait," calls out the bartender, overcome with curiosity. "Why did you smash the pack of chips over your head? I must know."

The hockey fan replies, "Because you didn't have any hot dogs. GO, HABS, GO!"

Help Me, Officer

A small boy gets lost at a hockey game. He goes up to a police officer and says, "I've lost my dad."

"What's he like?" the concerned officer asks sympathetically.

"Beer and women," says the boy.

A hockey coach who has an ulcer visits his doctor in the city.

"Remember," says the doctor, "don't get excited, don't get angry and forget about hockey when you're not down at the rink." Then he adds, "By the way, how could you let Johnson in net instead of Price with the season on the line like that? Geez! Now remember, no hockey."

Boss Check

A boss says to one of his employees, "I know you were playing hooky yesterday. You were out playing hockey."

"That a lie!" insists the employee. "And I have the fish to prove it!"

A Montreal woman, unable to bear the indifference of her hockey-obsessed husband now that the game has returned, yells at him, "You love the Canadiens more than you love me!"

He turns around and replies, "No, honey. I love the Maple Leafs more than I love you."

Cold Argument

Three macho hockey players in Winnipeg—one from Canada, one from Russia and the other from Finland—are sitting in the locker room arguing about who has the coldest climate. Certain he would clinch the argument, the Finn says that it is so cold in Finland the bed sheets freeze solid.

"*Nyet*, Russia is colder," says the Russian. "In Mother Russia, it is so cold that when we take shower, it snows."

"Pretty cold, boys," concedes the Canadian, "but I think we Canucks have got you beat." At that point he goes outside and returns with what looks like a frozen brown chunk of water. As the other two hockey players look at the object strangely, the Canadian says, "Frozen fart. I win."

Said by a veteran referee to a rookie partner working his first game:

"Remember, kid..when that puck drops, you and I will be the only two sane people in this rink."

A Little Fun for the Refs

When you're a ref, you have to face the fact that everyone hates you. After the end of the lockout, the refs did get some love from the fans but once hockey started again, it all went downhill from there. The fans hate you, the players hate you and the owners hate you. If you're a referee, you're about as popular as a rattlesnake in a jockstrap. There is only one way to stay sane and happy as a referee. It's not about love of the sport, and it's not about impartiality. It's all about knowing how much you're hated and getting revenge. The best way to do this is to get your digs in first. Here are my rules for having a fun, relaxing and, above all, vengeful time as a referee.

☛ Never read any interviews with players. They tend to criticize the standard of refereeing in this country, and you really don't need to see that kind of thing.

☛ Decide on your penalty ratio. This is the ratio of penalties during the game compared to the number of times you actually blow your whistle. Most NHL referees think a penalty ratio of 3:1 keeps the game flowing and saves them having to work too hard.

☛ Change your first name to "Ohgodits." Then, when you skate onto the ice at the beginning of a match and half the crowd says "Oh god, it's Smith" (assuming your name is Smith), it'll just sound like they're shouting your name.

☛ In the referee's dressing room before the game, toss a coin and decide which side you're going to show bias toward. It really winds the fans up. Note: you may want to simply choose the away side, so that all the home fans will get wound up at you. They are a much larger—and therefore more satisfying—groups to anger.

☛ Never wave at the fans when you skate out before the match. It only upsets them.

☛ Practice ignoring people. The fans will shout at you, and the players will shout at you, and it's best if you can ignore all of them. (Referees still living at home with their mothers believe that this is a very valuable skill and have plenty of chance to practice it.)

Late For Dinner

A wife is becoming increasingly annoyed by the fact that her hockey-playing husband is always home late from practice. Every night he promises he will be home in time for dinner, but something always arises to keep him at the rink later than planned. Consequently, night after night, she ends up throwing his dinner away. Eventually she gets so mad that she issues him an ultimatum: "Tonight you get home at six o'clock sharp or it's the last meal I ever cook for you."

Q: If a hockey player gets athletes foot, what does an astronaut get?

A: Missile toe.

The husband is worried. He loves his wife dearly but can't help staying late down at the rink. After all, he is trying to make it into the NHL and he needs to work. But he decides to make it home on time, for once. So he leaves the rink early, but as he crosses the street to get to the parking lot, he is hit by a car. He is rushed to the hospital, but his injuries turn out to be minor and he is discharged shortly afterward. Nevertheless, the delay means that it is eight o'clock before he arrives home.

His wife is raging mad. "What time do you call this? You promised me you'd be home by six!"

"Darling, I can explain. I know I'm late, but I was run over by a car."

"So what?" she says. "It takes two hours to get run over?"

New Life

A hockey player excitedly runs into his house one morning and yells to his girlfriend. "Sarah, pack up your stuff. I just signed a multi-million dollar contract!"

"That's great! Shall I pack for warm weather or cold?" she asks.

"Whatever. Just as long as you're out of the house by noon."

New Name

Following his first game in the NHL, Montreal Canadiens forward Alex Galchenyuk is being interviewed by the press.

"What's your name, kid?" asks a reporter.

"Galchenyuk, Alex."

"How do you spell it?" asks another reporter.

"A-L-E-X, Alex."

"No, not Alex. The last name."

"G-A-L-L, no, G-A-L-S, no, G-O-L, no, ah forget it. Just look at the back of my jersey."

New Money

To celebrate signing his first pro hockey contract, a rookie goes out and buys the best car available: a 1999 Ferrari GTO. It is the most expensive car in the world, and it costs him $500,000. He takes it out for a spin and stops for a red light.

> Why is a puck called a puck? Because dirty little bastard was taken.
>
> –Martin Brodeur

An old man on a moped (both looking about 75 years old) pulls up next to him. The old man looks over at the sleek, shiny car and asks, "What kind of car ya' got there, sonny?"

The young man replies, "A 1999 Ferrari GTO. It cost half a million dollars!"

"That's a lot of money," says the old man. "Why does it cost so much?"

BACK TO HOCKEY!!!   163

"Because this car can do up to 320 miles an hour!" states the young dude proudly.

The moped driver asks, "Mind if I take a look inside?"

"No problem," replies the owner.

So the old man pokes his head in the window and looks around. Sitting back on his moped, the old man says, "That's a pretty nice car, all right."

Just then the light changes, so the rookie decides to show the old man just what his car can do. He floors it, and within 30 seconds the speedometer reads 160 mph. Suddenly, he notices a dot in his rear view mirror. It seems to be getting closer. He slows down to see what it could be and suddenly, *whhhoooossshhh,* something whips by him, going much faster!

"What on earth could be going faster than my Ferrari?" the young man asks himself.

Then, ahead of him, he sees a dot coming toward him. *Whooooosh!* It goes by again, heading the opposite direction, and it looks like the old man on the moped!

"Couldn't be," mutters the guy. "How could a moped outrun a Ferrari?"

But again, he sees a dot in his rear view mirror. *Whooooosh, Ka-bblaMMM!* It plows into the back of his car, demolishing the rear end.

The young man jumps out, and it IS the old man! He runs up to the mangled old man and says, "Oh my god! Is there anything I can do for you?"

The old man whispers, "Unhook...my suspenders...from your side-view mirror...."

Compare and Contrast

A couple is on their honeymoon, lying in bed, about ready to consummate their marriage, when the new bride says to the husband, "I have a confession. I'm not a virgin."

The husband replies, "That's no big thing in this day and age."

The wife continues, "Yeah, I've been with one guy."

"Oh yeah? Who was the guy?"

"Sidney Crosby."

"Sidney Crosby, the hockey player?"

"Yeah."

"Well, he's rich, famous and handsome. I can see why you went to bed with him."

The husband and wife then make passionate love. When they are done, the husband gets up and walks to the telephone.

"What are you doing?" asks the wife.

The husband says, "I'm hungry. I was going to call room service and get something to eat."

"Sidney wouldn't do that."

"Oh yeah? What would Sidney do?"

"He'd come back to bed and do it a second time."

The husband puts down the phone and goes back to bed to make love a second time.

When they finish, he gets up and goes over to the phone. "Now what are you doing?" she asks.

The husband says, "I'm still hungry so I was going to call room service to get something to eat."

"Sidney wouldn't do that."

"Oh yeah? What would Sidney do?"

"He'd come back to bed and do it again."

The guy slams down the phone, goes back to bed and makes love one more time.

When they finish, he's beat. He drags himself over to the phone and starts to dial.

The wife asks, "Are you calling room service?"

"No! I'm calling Sidney Crosby to find out how many times I have to score to win this game."

◄ CHAPTER 8 ►

Fun With Hockey

With all the heavy, serious discussions about revenue sharing, players salaries and people losing their jobs because of the lockouts, it is nice to just lean back and have a good laugh at the game's expense.

NHLPA Telethon

Hundreds of National Hockey League players in our very own country are living at or just below the seven-figure salary level (atrocious!). And, as if that weren't bad enough, they will be deprived of pay for several weeks—possibly a whole year—as a result of the current lockout situation. But now, you can help!

For only $20,835 a month, about $694.50 a day (that's less than the cost of a large screen projection TV), you can help a hockey player remain economically viable during his time of need. This contribution by no means solves the problem, as it barely covers the yearly league minimum—but it's a start!

Almost $700 may not seem like a lot of money to you, but to a hockey player it could mean the difference between a vacation spent golfing in Florida or a Mediterranean cruise. For you, $700 is nothing more than one month's rent or mortgage payment. But to a hockey player, $700 will almost replace his daily salary.

Your commitment of just under $700 a day will enable a player to buy that home entertainment center, trade in the year-old Lexus for a new Ferrari or enjoy a weekend in Rio.

Each month, you will receive a complete financial report on the player you sponsor.

Detailed information about his stocks, bonds, 401(k), real estate and other investment holdings will be mailed to your home.

You'll also get information about how he plans to invest the $5 million lump sum he will receive upon retirement.

Q: *What's the best thing about concussions?*

A: *You keep meeting new friends.*

Plus upon signing up for this program, you will receive a photo of the player (unsigned—for a signed photo, please include an additional $50). Put the photo on your refrigerator to remind you of other people's suffering.

Your hockey player will be told that he has a SPECIAL FRIEND who just wants to help in a time of need. Although the player won't know your name, he will be able to make collect calls to your home via a special operator just in case additional funds are needed for unexpected expenses.

If you want to help, please send back the following form:

YES, I WANT TO HELP!

I would like to sponsor a striking NHL hockey player. My preference is checked below:

- ☐ Starter
- ☐ Reserve
- ☐ Star (Higher cost)
- ☐ Superstar (Much higher cost)
- ☐ Entire team (Please call our 900 number to ask for the cost of a specific team; cheerleaders not included.)
- ☐ I'll sponsor a player most in need. Please select one for me.

Please charge the account listed below $694.50 per day for a reserve player or starter for the duration of the strike. Please send me a picture of the player I have sponsored, along with a team logo and my very own NHL Players Association badge to wear proudly on my lapel.

Note: Sponsors are not permitted to contact the player they have sponsored, either in person or by other means including, but not limited to, telephone calls, letters, e-mail or third parties. Keep in mind that the hockey player you have sponsored will be much too busy enjoying his free time, thanks to your generous donations.

Contributions are not tax-deductible.

Thank you for your support of an athlete during the hockey lockout!

FUN WITH HOCKEY 169

News Flash: This just in! NHL locks out EA Sports teams, and all video game players have gone to play in Europe. Xboxes and Playstations across North America sit idle.

Just Like the Real Thing

Video game fans everywhere lined up to buy the latest hockey game. Hockey fans were excited to try the new features like contract negotiations, where players' deft moves at the conference table will surely excite. In this new hockey game, you can either play as the owners or the players. Finish the game on easy level and unlock the Gary Bettman character.

Locker Room Bet

Marion Hossa and Patrick Kane are in the dressing room after a game, just talking. When Hossa gets up to shower, Kane turns to a rookie on the team and says, "I bet you $1000 you've got a terrible case of hemorrhoids."

Knowing he doesn't have hemorrhoids, the rookie happily agrees to the bet, stands up, and pulls his pants down in the middle of the dressing room. Kane looks quickly and doesn't find a single hemorrhoid, so

> My message to the kids and our fans is hockey's a great game. There's a lot of hockey being played at all levels. Get involved, do it. We will be back and we will be back better than ever and hopefully as soon as possible. Don't give up on the game. It's too good.
>
> –Gary Bettman

he promptly hands over $1000. Smiling, he goes to take his shower. The rookie sits back down, and when Hossa returns, he happily tells the story of his winnings.

To the rookie's surprise, Hossa says, "That son-of-bitch! Just 10 minutes ago, he bet me $3000 he'd have you drop your pants in the middle of the dressing room."

Did you hear about the blonde who lost $50 on the hockey game? She lost $25 on the game and $25 on the replay.

Forever Love

Henrik Lundqvist comes home from the arena and asks his wife, "If I were, say, disfigured, would you still love me?"

"Darling, I will always love you," she says calmly while filing her nails.

"How about if I became impotent, losing my sex drive, and I could no longer make sweet love to you?"

"Don't worry about that, honey. I will always love you," she tells him, gently stroking his cheek.

"Well, how about if I sustain an injury and I lose my job as goaltender for the New York Rangers, thereby losing my million-dollar contract. Would you still love me then?"

His wife looks over at her husband's worried face. "Henrik, I will always love you," she reassures him, "but most of all, I'll really miss you."

Negotiated

Greztky is just about to leave the house to meet with team owners to renegotiate his contract when his daughter Paulina says, "Have a great day, Dad!"

"Thank you, sweetheart. But why did you say that?"

"Because if you have a great day, I'll have a great day."

Pauline Marois decides to retire from politics and move to Spain to get away from it all. Once she is settled, she gets into a conversation with her neighbor, who turns out to be as opinionated and outspoken as she is.

> Hockey: the only time men want to wear protection.

The neighbor exclaims, "So, you come from Quebec. I understand hockey is the most popular sport in Quebec. In Spain, we find it barbaric."

"Madame," says Marois. "I am surprised by your words. After all, in your country the most popular sport is bullfighting. Quebecers find that sport more than barbaric. And you also expressed that hockey is the most popular sport in Quebec. You are wrong on both accounts madam. Hockey is not Quebec's most popular sport—rebelling is."

Heavenly Hockey

Jesus, Moses and an old man are playing three on three shinny hockey against some angels on heaven's ice rink. In the first period, Moses gets the puck in his own end, speeds his way up the ice, past the angel forwards in the neutral zone, dekes out the defenseman and slaps a bullet that separates the ice in two and passes the goaltender.

Not to be out done, in the second period, Jesus takes the puck in his own end and skates slowly up the ice, completely untouched, because the opposing angels are awed by his heavenly glow. Jesus then puts the puck in the net without breaking a sweat.

Celebrity Death Match we all want to watch: the Hanson Brothers vs. Hanson (think "MMMBop")

In the third period, the old man takes the puck in his end and shoots it into the air. It travels off into space, then shoots down to the rink in a ball of flame. He snaps his fingers and disappears, then reappears in front of the goaltender only to pass through him like a ghost along with the puck for the game-winning goal.

Jesus turns to the old man and says, "Nice goal, Dad."

Message to Americans from Canadians

We will explain the appeal of hockey to you, if you Americans can explain the appeal of the National Rifle Association (NRA) to us!

A guy is on an outdoor rink playing hockey by himself when he slaps the puck over the boards and into the woods. He goes to get the puck and is startled to stumble upon a witch stirring a huge cauldron. Observing the steaming brew with fascination, he asks, "What's in there?"

"It's a magic brew," she says. "One swig and you'll play better hockey than anyone in the world. You'll be unstoppable."

"Awesome," he says. "Let me have some."

"Wait! Hold your horses, big boy," replies the old lady. "There's a catch. You'll be the greatest hockey player in the world, but you will have the worst sex life in all of Canada."

The man, having been married for 10 years, stops to think about it. "No sex, great hockey…" he ponders. "Give me the damn cup."

Finding his puck, the hockey player heads out of the woods and continues playing. He notices that his skills have greatly improved. His skating is incredible and his shot is powerful and precise. Soon he is recruited by an NHL team. He beats all of Gretzky's single-season records and leads his team to the Stanley Cup.

The following year, he returns to the same outdoor rink, walks into the woods and is surprised to see the same witch stirring her pot of boiling brew.

"You again," she wheezes. "How's your hockey game?"

He tells her about his various exploits on the ice and about winning the Stanley Cup.

"And your sex life?" The witch smiles malevolently, but her expression quickly changes when he answers, "Better than it was."

"Better than it was? How many times did you get laid this year?"

"Three, maybe four times," answered the husband.

At the Game

A priest and a rabbi go to a hockey game at Madison Square Garden. At one point, two players drop their gloves to fight. One of the does the sign of the cross before throwing the first punch.

"What does that mean?" asks the rabbi.

"Not a damn thing if he can't fight," answers the priest.

Two men are warming up to play tennis when one man notices that the other has bruised shins.

"Those look like they're in pretty bad shape. You play hockey?"

"No," replies the other man, "I tried watching hockey on my wife's birthday."

It is a boring day in the jungle, so the elephants decide to challenge the monkeys to a floor hockey game. The game is going well with the elephants beating the monkeys 10–0, when suddenly the monkeys start making a comeback.

> If hockey and exercise are so good for your health, why do the professionals retire by age 35?

The monkeys' star player has the ball and is moving up through the neutral zone when he dekes his way past the defense (which is a feat for a monkey against an elephant), and he is just about to put the puck past the goaltender when one of the elephants comes lumbering in from behind and steps on the monkey, killing him instantly.

The referee stops the game. "What the hell did you do that for? Do you call that sportsmanship to kill another player?"

The elephant replies, "Well, I didn't mean to kill him—I was just trying to trip him."

Class Exercise

As an exercise in history class one day, each student is to list who they consider to be the six greatest Canadians of all time. After a half an hour, everyone in the class has turned in their papers except for Mike, who is still scratching his head and thinking furiously.

"What's up?" asks the teacher. "Can't you come up with six great Canadians?"

"I've got all but one," the student replies hastily. "It's the goaltender I can't decide on."

> **Q:** What do you get when you rearrange Jaromir?
> **A:** Mario Jr.

A hockey fan is a guy who will yell at a forward for not spotting the open winger, then head for the parking lot and not be able to find his own car.

Truly Over

My neighbor is crying because her husband has left her for the sixth time. I try to console her, saying, "Don't worry, he'll be back."

"Not this time," she replies. "He's taken his hockey gear."

A stranger walks into a Winnipeg Jets bar and announces loudly, "Hey, guys, have I got some great hockey player jokes for you."

The bartender leans over and says in an ominous tone, "Listen, if I were you I'd watch your tongue. The two 300-pound bouncers are hockey players, I'm no midget and I'm a hockey player, and so is every other guy in here."

"Oh, no problem," replies the stranger cheerfully. "I'll just speak v-e-r-y s-l-o-w-l-y, t-h-e-n."

Sorry Gift

A man and his wife are having an argument in bed. The husband has finally had enough, so he jumps up and takes a blanket to the couch.

The next day, the wife feels bad about what happened and decides to buy her husband a gift. Because he is an avid hockey player, she goes to the pro shop down the street.

The wife talks to the salesman, and he suggests a new graphite stick and shows her one of his finest. "How much is it?" she asks.

"It's $250," he replies. She thinks that is kind of expensive and tells him so.

"But it comes with an inscription," the salesman says.

"What kind of inscription?" she asks.

"Whatever you wish," he explains. "But, one of the old hockey favorites is: 'Play Hard, No Excuses.'"

"Oh, that will never do!" exclaims the wife. "That's what started the argument in the first place."

Hockey Dads

Four guys are playing in their old-timer league. Three of the guys are getting changed while the other is in the shower. Naturally, they start talking about their sons.

"My son Kent," says one, "has made quite a name for himself in the home-building industry. He began as a carpenter but now owns his own design and construction firm. He's so successful, in fact, that in the last year he was able to give a good friend a brand new home as a gift."

The second man, not to be outdone, tells how his son began his career as a car salesman but now owns a multi-line dealership. "Norm's so successful that, in the last six months, he gave his friend two brand new cars as a gift."

The third man's son, Greg, has worked his way up through a stock brokerage and in the last few weeks has given a good friend a large stock portfolio as a gift.

When the fourth man gets back from the shower, the other men tell him that they have been discussing their progeny and ask what line his son is in.

"To tell the truth, I'm not very pleased with how my son turned out," he replies. "For 15 years, Chico's been a hairdresser, and I've just recently discovered he's gay. However, on the bright side, he must be good

Q: *What do you get when you rearrange Tie Domi?*

A: *Me idiot.*

at what he does because his last three boyfriends have given him a brand new house, two cars and a big pile of stock certificates."

> **Q:** How do hockey players stay cool?
> **A:** They sit next to their fans.

Half an hour before hockey practice, a player walks into the medical room and says, "Doc, I hurt all over."

Even though it is the doctor's first day on the job, he is not naive enough to believe the player so he says, "That's impossible. You're just trying to get the day off, right?"

"No, really, I hurt all over," the player insists. "Look, when I touch my arm—ouch. When I touch my leg—ouch. When I touch my chest—ouch. When I touch my head—ouch."

The doctor nods and asks, "You've had more than 10 concussions, haven't you?"

The player looks puzzled and then says, "Yes, how did you know?"

The doctor replies, "Because your finger is broken."

Mammals vs. Insects

A team of mammals is playing a team of insects. The mammals totally dominated the first half of the hockey game and are leading 28–0. However, about one hour into the game, the insects make a substitution and bring on a centipede. The centipede scores an incredible 200 goals, and the insects win the game by a final score of 200–28. In the dressing room after the game, the captain of the mammals is chatting to the insect captain.

"That centipede of yours is terrific," says the mammals' captain. "Why didn't you play him from the start?"

"We would have liked to," says the insects' captain, "but it takes him at least 45 minutes to get his skates on."

Top 20 Pet Peeves of Hockey Goaltenders

20. Drunk fans who toss Hostess Ding Dongs toward the net.

19. Players at parties who want to turn the mask upside down and fill it up with bean dip.

18. Pads make it look like they have really big butts.

17. T-shirts that say, "Goaltenders do it with their glove hand."

16. They will not have a good reason for dropping anything ever again.

15. Frostbite caused by a leg split.

14. When the trainer fills the water bottle with Folgers Crystals.

13. Goal judges at away games who constantly make wisecracks about "burning out the goal lamp."

12. Fans who ask, "Can I have your autograph, Mr. Roy?" (pronounced like it's spelled)

11. Jealous backup goalies that follow them around in the locker room screaming, "Hey, glove THIS, pal!"

10. Smart-asses who toss beach balls at the net.

9. Letting those beach balls in.

8. Jealous backup goalies that hide your cup, causing "puck castration."

7. Always-annoying death threats from opposition upon stopping a 2-on-1.

6. Always-annoying death threats from teammates upon letting in a 2-on-1.

5. Always-annoying death threats from fans upon stepping onto the ice.

4. Laser pointers in the face.

3. Being a top-rated NHL goalie, being traded to a cold Canadian city, not getting the money you deserve, and having to play in Las Vegas (Curtis Joseph only).

2. The opposite sex just doesn't understand why you have to wear a mask to bed.

1. When you flip the ref the bird behind the blocker, they can't even tell.

Hockey Knowledge

Patricia is beginning her job as a school counselor and is keen to help the students. One day during recess, she notices a girl standing all by herself on one side of the playing field while the rest of the children are enjoying a game of hockey at the other end of the playground. Patricia goes up to the girl and asks if she is all right. The girl says that she is fine. Some time later, however, Patricia notices that the girl is in exactly the same spot, still by herself.

Going up to her again, the school counselor asks, "Would you like me to be your friend?"

The girl hesitates, then says, "All right," while looking at Patricia with some suspicion.

Feeling she is making some progress, Patricia then asks, "Why are you standing here all alone?"

"Because," the girl says with a large sigh, "duh! I'm the goalie!"

Diagnosis

A health teacher has just finished a lecture on mental health and gives the class an oral quiz. Speaking specifically about depression, the teacher asks, "How would you diagnose a person who walks back and forth screaming at the top of his lungs one minute, then sits down weeping uncontrollably the next?"

Q: What is the best way to get a hockey player into a bank?

A: Offer free checking.

A young student sitting in the rear of the classroom raises his hand and says, "A hockey dad?"

A recent poll reports that the more intelligent a person is, the less he watches hockey. Personally, I think they have it backward: the more a person watches hockey, the less intelligent he becomes.

Trade

A Canadian hockey player is walking down the street with a case of beer under his arm. His friend Doug stops him and asks, "Hey Bobby! Whatcha get the case of beer for?"

"I got it for my wife, eh," answers Bobby.

"Oh!" exclaims Doug. "Good trade."

Martin Brodeur goes to a casino. He puts a dollar in the soda machine, and a Coke comes out. He does it one more time and gets a Sprite. He is about to put in another quarter, but Henrik Lundqvist is behind him and says, "Hey, it is my turn now!"

Marty turns to Lundqvist and says, "You're just jealous because I'm on a winning streak."

Communication Breakdown

A Chinese businessman decides to visit a newly acquired business in Canada. As a gesture of goodwill, the executives of his newly acquired business take him to a hockey rink to teach him the game he has never seen.

Upon his return to China, his family asks what he did in Canada. He replies, "Played most interesting game. Hit little black puck with long stick on frozen water. Name of game is 'sh*t.'"

Court Choice

A child stands in court before a judge. His parents are divorcing and the judge is asking him which parent he would prefer to live with. "Would you like to live with your mother?" the judge asks.

"No! She beats me every night. I don't want to live with her!"

So the judge says, "Okay, you can go live with your dad, then."

The child replies, "No! He beats me every night, as well! I don't want to live with him!"

The judge says, "Well, if both your parents beat you, then who do you want to live with?"

The boy replies, "The Toronto Maple Leafs."

The judge is puzzled. "Why would you want to live with them?" he asks.

The boy replies, "Because they don't beat anyone!"

Two boys are playing hockey at an outdoor arena in Calgary when one is attacked by a pitbull. Thinking quickly, the other boy rips a board off the nearby fence, wedges it down the dog's collar and twists, breaking the dog's neck. A reporter who is walking by sees the incident and rushes over to interview the boy.

"Calgary Flames fan saves friend from vicious animal," he starts writing in his notebook.

"But I'm not a Flames fan," the boy says.

FUN WITH HOCKEY   185

"Oh, okay. How about 'Edmonton Oilers fan rescues friend from horrific attack,'" the reporter says.

"I'm not an Oilers fan either," the boy says.

"Then what are you?" the reporter asks.

"I'm a Maple Leafs fan."

The reporter turns to a new sheet in his notebook and writes, "Redneck idiot kills family pet."

Adultery

One evening, a guy heads out to the store to buy a pack of cigarettes for his wife. The store is closed, so he goes to a nearby bar to have a drink and bum a smoke off someone. As he sits down at the bar, he notices a stunning brunette perched on the next stool. He can't believe how gorgeous she is, so he starts chatting with her. He buys her a drink— and another, and another— and when the bar closes, she invites him back to her apartment.

When they reach her apartment, they go straight to bed. The sex is fantastic. Afterward, he looks at his watch and sees that it is 3:00 AM.

"Jesus Christ!" he exclaims, leaping out of bed. "I didn't realize it was so late. My wife's gonna kill me. Have you got any hockey tape?"

The girl looks puzzled but hands him the tape, which he puts in his pocket. Then without saying a word, he quickly leaves.

Back home, his wife is waiting for him. "Where have you been?" she demands angrily. "Do you know what time it is? I sent you out for a packet of cigarettes, and you've been gone nearly seven hours!"

"Look, honey, I'm really sorry," he says. "I went to the store for your cigarettes but the store was shut. So I went to the bar next door to see if they had one of those old vending machines, which they didn't, so I decided to have a beer. While I was there, I met this great-looking chick, and we ended up in bed together, and I had the most wild, passionate sex."

"Let me see what's in your pockets," she says, and he shows her. "You liar!" she screams, seeing the tape. "You were playing hockey again!"

Ouch Lady

A little old lady is walking down the street dragging two plastic garbage bags with her, one in each hand. There is a hole in one of the bags, and it is leaving a trail of $20 bills on the sidewalk. Spotting this, a police officer stops the old lady.

"Ma'am, there are $20 bills falling out of that bag of yours," he says.

"Damn!" she replies. "I'd better go back and get them. Thanks for the warning, officer."

"Well now, not so fast," says the cop. "How did you get all that money? Did you rob a bank or something?"

"Oh, heavens no," replies the old lady. "You see, my garden backs onto an arena, and each time there is a hockey game, afterward a lot of fans come and pee in the bushes, right onto my prized garden. So I go and stand behind the bushes with a big pair of shears, and each time someone sticks his thingie through the bushes I say, '$20 or it comes off!'"

"Hey, not a bad idea," laughs the cop. "Okay, good luck! By the way, what's in the other bag?"

"Not everyone pays up...."

Top 10 Best Things About Being a Hockey Goaltender

10. Halloween costume? No problem!

9. Detroit Red Wing goalies look like Santa and can earn extra money during the holidays.

8. You can check out the babes (or guys) rink-side without them even knowing.

7. Slash all you want; someone else gets sent to the box.

6. The padding gives the impression you're really buffed.

5. The helmet allows you to double as Darth Vader in any upcoming *Star Wars* films.

4. You can get an inventive nickname like "Eddie."

3. Flexibility can be useful in other entertainment ventures, if you know what I mean.

2. Bruises can really bring out the color of your eyes.

1. Two words: bigger stick.

Hockey Dummies

Two dumb hockey enforcers decide to go duck hunting. Neither one of them has ever been hunting before and after several hours they still haven't bagged any.

One hunter looks at the other and says, "I just don't understand it—why aren't we getting any ducks?"

His friend says, "I keep telling you, I just don't think we're throwing the dog high enough."

Two inner-city Toronto boys are playing with new sticks and pucks in the park near their house.

"Hey," shouts their mother, "where did you get that equipment?"

"We found it," replies one of the boys.

"Are you sure it was lost?" asks the mother.

"Yes," replies the boy. "We saw some people looking for it just a while ago."

Christmas

A father asks his son what he would like for Christmas.

"I've got my eye on those special goalie pads in the sports store window," replies the young lad.

"The $500 ones?" asks the father.

"That's right."

"You'd better keep your eye on them then, because it's unlikely you're ever gonna wear them," says the dad firmly.

One of the Columbus Blue Jackets' best players is called as a character witness in a divorce case and, on being asked his profession, replies, "I am the greatest hockey player in the world!"

After the case is over, he gets a good deal of teasing from his teammates. "How could you stand up in court and say a thing like that?" they ask.

"Well," he replies. "You must remember I was under oath."

Schooled

A friendly hockey game is set to take place in Montreal between a group of McGill University students and a team made up of teaching assistants and professors. Before the game, the two designated captains meet on the ice to exchange pleasantries.

They shake hands, and the student leader says, "May the best team win!"

The university captain, a professor of English, replies, "You mean, may the better team win!"

> Q: Why doesn't Jesus like hockey?
> A: Cause he's not special. Everyone is walking on water.

Out Shopping

Sidney Crosby is out shopping and discovers a new brand of Olympic condoms. Clearly impressed, he buys a pack. Upon getting home he tells his girlfriend about the purchase he just made.

"Olympic condoms?" she blurts. "What makes them so special?"

"There are three colors," he replies. "Gold, silver and bronze."

"What color are you going to wear tonight?" she asks cheekily.

"Gold, of course," says Sidney proudly. The girlfriend responds, "Really? Why don't you wear silver? It would be nice if you came second for a change."

Two hockey fans are in court for fighting. One fan bit off part of the other's ear, and the judge fines him $600.

"But it was self-defense," the fan complains.

The judge ignores him. "You're fined $600 and bound to keep the peace for a year."

"I can't do that," says the fan. "I threw it in a dustbin."

Canadian Fisherman

James Reimer of the Toronto Maple Leafs is an avid fisherman. One day he decides to cross the

FUN WITH HOCKEY   191

Peace Bridge to Lewiston and fish the American side of the Niagara River.

He settles down on a quiet dock and is filling his bucket with some nice fish when an American game warden approaches him and says, "May I see your fishing license please?"

When Reimer hands over his license, the game warden says that it is no good because it is a Canadian fishing license.

At this point Reimer says, "But I'm only catching Canadian fish."

The warden scratches his head for a moment and finally asks, "What do you mean?"

Reimer reaches in his bucket, pulls out a fish and asks the warden, "What kind of fish is this?"

The warden takes a look and says, "It's a smallmouth bass."

Reimer replies, "See what I mean? If it was an American fish, it would be a largemouth bass."

Fishy Pets

During the off-season, Chris Pronger is fishing at a lake in northern Ontario that he's never had any luck on, but on this day he is catching a fish on almost every cast. When he is done for the day, he realizes he caught more than the law allows, but he decides to keep them all anyway. Just as he finishes packing the fish in his car and is about to drive away, the game warden pulls up and asks to see his fish.

When Pronger reluctantly shows the warden his fish, the warden says, "You've caught too many."

Pronger calmly says, "Those fish are not from the lake. They are my pet fish, and everyday I bring them down to the lake so they can get some food and exercise."

The warden, not believing a word of the story says, "How do you get them back?"

Pronger explains that he simply whistles and they jump into the bucket one by one.

Well, the warden, having heard every excuse in the book, says he wants to see Pronger call the fish back. So the two men go out to the water's edge. The warden tells Pronger to let the fish go, and Pronger dumps the fish into the lake. After a couple of minutes, the warden tells him to whistle and get the fish back.

Pronger replies, "What fish?"

A Visit

A hockey player with terrible back problems is forced to go to a chiropractor even though he doesn't believe in the treatments they offer. Reluctantly he gets on the examination table and lets the chiropractor get to work. Half an hour later, he gets up and his problem is completely cured.

"So," says the chiropractor, "how do you feel about us chiropractors now?"

The hockey player says, "I stand corrected."

Carey Price, a noted hunter, and his buddy Colby Armstrong rent a moose costume hoping they can get close enough to a bull moose to kill it. They creep up on a huge bull moose but find that the costume's zipper is stuck. Suddenly there is a loud bellow and Price, in the front of the costume, sees that the bull moose is approaching them with a huge erection.

"What are we going to do now?" asks Armstrong, in the back of the costume.

"I'm going to nibble some grass," replies Price. "You'd better brace yourself."

Sneaky

Three Canadians and three Americans are traveling to a hockey game. The three Americans each buy tickets then watch as the three Canadians buy only one.

"How are the three of you going to travel on only one ticket?" asks an American.

"Watch and you'll see," says a Canadian.

They all board the train. The Americans take their respective seats, but all three Canadians cram into a bathroom and close the door behind them.

Shortly after the train has departed, the conductor comes around collecting tickets. He knocks on the bathroom door and says, "Ticket, please!" The door opens a crack, and a single arm emerges with a ticket in hand. The conductor takes it and moves on. The Americans see this and agree it is quite a clever idea.

So after the game, they decide to copy the Canadians on the return trip and save some money. When they get to the station, they buy a single ticket for the return trip. To their astonishment the Canadians don't buy a ticket at all.

"How are you going to travel without a ticket?" asks one perplexed American.

"Watch and you'll see," replies a Canadian.

When they board the train the three Americans cram into a bathroom, and nearby the three Canadians cram into another bathroom.

Once the train leaves the station, one of the Canadians leaves their bedroom and walks over to the other bathroom where the Americans are hiding, knocks on the door and says, "Ticket, please!"

CHAPTER 9

More Fun with Hockey

There are too many jokes about everyone's favorite game on ice to fill just one chapter, so here are some more to give you a chuckle and get you smiling about hockey again, instead of cursing or crying over it.

Wayward Shot

After a particularly poor game of golf, Patrick Sharp of the Chicago Blackhawks skips the clubhouse and starts on his way home. As he is walking to the parking lot to get his car, a policeman stops him and asks, "Did you tee off on the 16th hole about 20 minutes ago?"

"Yes," Sharp responds.

"Did you happen to hook your ball so that it went over the trees and off the course?" the cop asks.

"Yes, I did. How did you know?" Sharp asks.

"Well," says the policeman very seriously, "your ball flew out onto the highway and crashed through a driver's windshield. The car went out of control, crashing into five other cars and a fire truck. The fire truck couldn't make it to the fire it was heading to, and the building burned down. So, what are you going to do about it?"

Sharp thinks it over carefully and responds, "I think I'll close my stance a little bit, tighten my grip and lower my right thumb."

Frenemies

There's no game like hockey. You go out with several friends, play three periods and return with enemies.

Two old friends are just about to play a game of pickup hockey in their neighborhood when a stranger comes up and asks if he can play.

"Sure," they say.

So they start playing and enjoy the game and the company of the newcomer. Partway through the game, one of the friends asks the newcomer, "What do you do for a living?"

"I'm a hit man," is the reply.

"You're joking!"

"No, I'm not," the newcomer says, reaching into his hockey bag and pulling out a beautiful sniper's rifle with a large telescopic sight. "Here are my tools."

"That's a beautiful telescopic sight," says the other friend. "Can I take a look? I think I might be able to see my house from here." He picks up the rifle and looks through the sight in the direction of his house.

MORE FUN WITH HOCKEY

197

"Yeah, I can see my house all right. This sight is fantastic. I can see right in the window. Wow, I can see my wife in the bedroom. Ha Ha, she's naked! What's that? Wait a minute, that's my neighbor in there with her. He's naked as well! That bitch!" He turns to the hitman. "How much do you charge for a hit?"

Hockey was once a rich man's sport, but now it has millions of poor players.

"I do a flat rate. For you, $1000 every time I pull the trigger."

"Can you do two for me now?"

"Sure, what do you want?"

"First, shoot my wife; she's always been mouthy, so shoot her in the mouth. Then the neighbor, he's a mate of mine, a bit of a lad, so just shoot his dick off to teach him a lesson."

The hitman grabs the rifle and takes aim, standing perfectly still for a few minutes.

"Are you going to do it or not?" asks the friend testily.

"Just wait a moment, be patient," says the hitman calmly. "I think I can save you a grand here...."

Hard to Choose

Star Flyers forward Claude Giroux is going out with three different girls at the same time. He wants to settle down but can't decide which of the three to ask to be his bride. So he decides to perform a test.

He will give each of the girls $5000 to spend and will monitor what each of them does with the money.

The first girl spends the cash on a complete makeover—new clothes, new hairdo, the lot. She tells him, "I wanted to look my best for you because I love you so much." He is impressed.

The second girl buys new golf clubs, an iPad, an expensive leather jacket and a new ultra high definition TV and gives them to him as gifts. "These are a token of my love for you," she declares. Again, he is impressed.

The third girl invests the $5000 in the stock market, triples her initial investment and gives him the $5000 back and reinvests the remainder, "For our future, because I love you so much." Once more he is impressed.

Clearly, it is a tough decision to choose between the three ladies. He spends several days in deep contemplation over what to do before finally coming to the only rational conclusion possible—he chooses the one with the biggest breasts.

Good Shooter

George Parros hits his ball 300 yards straight down the fairway, and it hits a sprinkler and careens off into the woods. He finds the ball, but trees surround it. He's pissed, figures what the hell, grabs his nine-iron, and hits the ball as hard as he can. It bounces off a tree back at his head and kills him.

George arrives in heaven, and God himself is at the Pearly Gates to greet him. Looking up his records, God sees that Parros plays golf as well as hockey and says, "Are you any good?"

George looks at God and says, "I got here in two, didn't I?"

Top 10 Reasons the Goaltender Just Let That One In

10. My defense and I got involved in the "tastes great, less filling" debate.

9. Tried to read the "vulcanized" label on the side of the puck.

8. Slipped on this damn ice; someone should get some salt on that!

7. Was still laughing at that last top 10 list.

6. Misunderstood "butterfly save"; now sad to report one less monarch flying around.

5. Sun was in my eyes.

4. Misunderstood use of trapper; let in a goal, but got a lovely fur coat.

3. Being a top-rated NHL goalie, being traded to a cold Canadian city, not getting the money you deserve and having to play in Las Vegas.

2. Wait, I'm the backup! Go talk to El-Sieve-o over there!

1. Yeah, like YOU would get in front of that!

The Practical Widow

A woman goes into the local newspaper office to see that the obituary for her recently deceased husband is published. The obit editor informs her that there is a charge of 50 cents per word. She pauses, reflects and then says, "Well, then, let it read 'Fred Brown died.'" Amused at the woman's thrift, the editor tells her that there is a seven-word minimum for all obituaries. She thinks it over and in a few seconds says, "In that case, let it read, 'Fred Brown died: hockey gear for sale.'"

It's a Trap

Woman: "Would you get married again if I died?"

Man: "Definitely not!"

Woman: "Why not? Don't you like being married?"

Man: "Of course, I do."

Woman: "Then why wouldn't you remarry?"

Man: "Okay, I'd get married again."

Woman: "You would?" (With a hurt look on her face)

Man: (audible groan)

Woman: "Would you sleep with her in our bed?"

Man: "Where else would we sleep?"

Woman: "Would you put away my pictures, and replace them with pictures of her?"

Man: "That would seem like the proper thing to do."

Woman: "And would you let her use my hockey sticks?"

Man: "She can't use them—she's left-handed."

Woman: (silence)

Man: "Sh*t."

One day, a man comes home and is greeted by his wife dressed in a very sexy nightie.

"Tie me up," she purrs, "and you can do anything you want."

So he ties her up and goes to play hockey.

So Many Penguins

Three hockey buddies die in an auto accident and go to heaven. Upon arrival, they notice the most beautiful arena they have ever seen. St. Peter tells them they are welcome to play on the ice, but he cautions them with one rule: "Don't step on the penguins."

The men have blank expressions on their faces, and finally one of them says, "The penguins?"

"Yes," says St. Peter. "There are millions of penguins walking around the rink, and when one of them is stepped on, he squawks, and then the one next to him squawks, and soon they're all raising

> Hockey is an expensive way of losing your teeth.

hell, and it really breaks the tranquility. If you step on the penguins, you'll be punished."

The men start playing on the ice, and within 15 minutes, one of the guys steps on a penguin. The penguin squawks, and soon there is a deafening roar of penguins squawking.

St. Peter appears with an extremely homely woman and asks, "Who stepped on a penguin?"

"I did," admits one of the men. St. Peter immediately pulls out a pair of handcuffs and cuffs the man to the homely woman.

"I told you not to step on the penguins," he says. "Now you'll be handcuffed together for eternity."

The two other men are very cautious not to step on any penguins, but a couple of weeks later, one of them accidentally does. The squawks are as deafening as before, and within minutes, St. Peter walks up with a woman who is even uglier than the last one. He determines who stepped on the penguin by seeing the fear in the man's face, and he cuffs him to the woman. "I told you not to step on the penguins," St. Peter says. "Now you'll be handcuffed together for eternity."

The third man is extremely careful. Some days he doesn't even move for fear of nudging a penguin. After three months of this, he still hasn't stepped on a penguin. St. Peter walks up to the man, and with him is the most beautiful woman the man has ever seen. St. Peter smiles and without a word, handcuffs him to the beautiful woman and walks off.

The man, knowing that he will be handcuffed to this woman for eternity, lets out a sigh and says, "What have I done to deserve this?"

The woman replies, "I don't know about you, but I stepped on a penguin."

Personal Ads

A 40-something business executive and avid hockey player is browsing the personal ads on the Internet when he comes across an interesting ad from an attractive lady living in the same town.

The ad reads as follows: Slim, attractive, buxom blonde, 5'6", 125 lbs. successful in business, happy in life, no children (or desire to have them), enjoys traveling, pampering her man and the finer things in life. Seeks similar qualities in a partner for long-term relationship. HOCKEY PLAYERS NEED NOT APPLY.

A couple of old guys are playing hockey when one says he is going to Dr. Taylor for a new set of dentures in the morning.

His friend remarks that he went to the same dentist a couple years before.

"Is that so?" the first says. "Did he do a good job?"

"Well, I was on the ice yesterday when a fellow took a wicked slap shot," he says. "The puck most have been going 200 mph when it hit me in the stomach. That was the first time in two years my teeth didn't hurt."

Hockey Lovers

There's a fellow who is an avid hockey player. Actually he's a hockey fanatic. Every Saturday morning he gets up early and plays hockey outside all day. Well, this one Saturday morning, he gets up early, dresses quietly, gets his gear out of the closet and goes out to his car to drive to the rink. It is raining a torrential downpour. There is snow mixed with the rain and the wind is blowing 50 mph.

He comes back into the house and turns the TV to the weather channel. He sees that it's supposed to be bad weather all day long. So he puts his gear back into the closet, quietly undresses and slips back into bed where he cuddles up to his wife's back and whispers, "The weather out there is terrible."

She replies, "I know. And can you believe my stupid husband is actually out there playing hockey?"

Two friends are discussing the finer points of the game of hockey.

"What I like about hockey," the first guy says, "is that you get to spend the day with your friends in the fresh air, exercising your body and mind."

"Screw that," says his friend. "I'll tell you why hockey is such a great game. Where else can a guy like me get to spend the day with a bunch of hookers and not have his wife kill him!"

Locker Room

A cell phone rings in the men's locker room at the local hockey rink.

"Hello?"

"Honey, it's me. Are you at the rink?"

"Yes, just finished showering."

"Great! I'm at the mall, and I just saw a beautiful leather coat that's on sale for $1000. May I buy it?"

"Well, go ahead if you like it that much."

"Thanks, honey. By the way, I also stopped by the Mercedes dealership and saw the 2013 models. I spoke with the salesman, and he quoted me a really good price on the one I love."

"How much?"

"Only $60,000."

"Okay, but tell him you'll only pay $59,500."

"Thanks, sweetie. I'll see you later. I love you!"

"I love you, too. Bye."

The man hangs up and closes the phone's flap. Then he yells across the locker room, "Anybody know whose phone this is?"

Cheating Wife

Bill and Shirley are celebrating their 50th wedding anniversary.

"Shirley, I was wondering—have you ever cheated on me?"

"Oh, Bill, why would you ask such a question now? You don't want to ask that question."

"Yes, Shirley, I really want to know. Please."

"Well, all right. Yes, three times."

"Three? When were they?"

"Well, Bill, remember when you were 35 years old and you really wanted to start the business on your own and no bank would give you a loan? Remember how one day the bank president himself came over to the house and signed the loan papers, no questions asked?"

"Oh, Shirley, you did that for me! I respect you even more than ever, that you would do such a thing for me! So, when was number two?"

"Well, Bill, remember when you had that last heart attack and you were needing that very tricky operation, and no surgeon would touch you? Remember how Dr. Johnson came all the way up here, to do the surgery himself, and then you were in good shape again?"

"I can't believe it! Shirley, I love that you would do such a thing for me, to save my life! I couldn't have a more wonderful wife. To do such a thing, you must really love me, darling. I couldn't be more moved. When was number three?"

"Well, Bill, remember a few years ago, when you really wanted to be president of the hockey association and you were 15 votes short?"

Faithful

A woman is cleaning out her attic and comes across a small box. She opens it and finds three pucks and $250.

When her husband comes home, she questions him, and he finally admits that every time he was unfaithful to her he put a puck in the box.

> In primitive society, when native tribes beat the ground with clubs and yelled, they were called insane. Today, in civilized society, it is called hockey.

She immediately goes ballistic and starts yelling at him, but as she is doing so she is thinking, *30 years of marriage and only three pucks.*

She calms down and says, "What you have done is not nice, but I forgive you. However, I still don't know what the $250 is all about."

Her husband looks up at her and timidly says, "Well darling, every time I collected a dozen pucks, I would sell them."

Jimmy's wife constantly nags him to teach her to play hockey. Finally, one morning he relents and he takes her to the rink. Out on the ice he stands in front of the net and says, "Now watch me, and do the same thing."

He hits a nice shot and it sails straight into the top corner of the net.

His wife steps up, drills it, hooks it and bounces it off the crossbar. It clips the boards, flies up into the rafters over the pair, rebounds back toward net and blasts through the net for the goal.

The husband looks at her in shock and says, "Okay, now you know how to play. Let's go home."

Our Marriage

It seems that, after all these years, the romance and love just isn't what it used to be for John and Jane. In an attempt to salvage their 30 years of marriage, Jane convinces her husband to see a marriage counselor with her.

The counselor first asks Jane what she feels the problem is, and before he has even finished his sentence, she goes into a tirade listing every single problem the couple has ever had—even before things went south. She goes on and on for nearly an hour, and finishes in tears.

Finally, the counselor gets up from his couch, walks over to Jane, embraces her and kisses her passionately. She quiets down immediately and sits there in a daze.

The counselor then turns to John and says, "Your wife needs this at least three times a week.

For the sake of your marriage, can you can do this?"

The husband ponders the question for a moment and replies, "I can drop her off here on Mondays and Wednesdays…but on Fridays, I play hockey."

A guy stood over the puck for what seemed an eternity; looking up, looking down, measuring the distance, figuring the direction and speed. He was driving his friends nuts. Finally his exasperated teammate says, "What's taking so long? Hit the blasted puck!"

The guy answers, "My wife is up there watching me from the stands. I want to make this a perfect shot."

"Forget it, man. You don't stand a snowball's chance in hell of hitting her from here!"

The Good Wife

Peter was not feeling well—bad enough that his wife, Sharon, had to go and get his test results from the doctor.

"Now, Sharon, I don't know exactly what the problem is. Peter may even die if he doesn't get the right treatment. The only thing is, the right treatment is going to seem a little strange. Peter needs to play hockey as often as he has strength, and you need to give him all the sex he can handle."

Sharon nods and leaves. When she gets home, Peter is anxious to find out about his test results.

"Well, Sharon, what did the doctor have to say?"

Sharon looked him straight in the face. "You're gonna die."

The Difference Between Religions

A Catholic, a Baptist and a Mormon are bragging about the size of their families.

"I have five boys and my wife is expecting another. One more son and I'll have a hockey team!" says the Catholic.

"That's nothing!" says the Baptist. "I have 10 boys now, and my wife is pregnant with another child. One more son and I'll have a football team!"

"You both should be ashamed of yourselves!" says the Mormon. "I have 17 wives. One more and I'll have a golf course!"

Hockey in Heaven

Bill and his wife, Sally, die and go to heaven together. They are met at the gates by an angel who shows them around. "Right over here, we have our very own arena!" he says.

"Wow! It's beautiful! Can we use it now?" they both ask.

"Sure!" says the angel.

So, the couple starts playing a game of hockey. It is the most beautiful arena they have ever seen.

Everything is perfect. The ice is smooth, the equipment is top of the line, and they even get to play all the dead greats. The more they play, the more the woman beams with happiness, but she notices her husband is becoming disheartened and angry.

Sally asks her husband what is wrong. She says, "I can't understand why you're not happy. We're in heaven! We're together! We're playing on the most perfect rink ever! What's wrong with you?"

Bill replies, "If you hadn't fed us those DAMN bran muffins, we'd have been here years ago!"

A Bruins fan dies and is met at the Pearly Gates by an angel who offers to show him around heaven. As they walk the grounds, the Bruins fan notices what looks like a hockey rink.

"Can we go inside?" he asks his guide.

"Sure," the angel replies.

When he enters the rink, the Bruins fan is struck by the sight of a lone skater going up and down the ice. The skater is graceful and fast, and he makes moves that seem impossible for mere mortals. And he has on a Bruins jersey with #4 on his back.

The Bruins fan turns to the angel with tears welling in his eyes and says, "Oh my God, that's Bobby Orr. When did he die?"

The angel replies, "He's not dead. That's God, but he thinks he's Bobby Orr."

Working It

In 1923, who was:

☛ President of the largest steel company?

☛ President of the largest gas company?

☛ President of the New York Stock Exchange?

☛ Greatest wheat speculator?

☛ President of the Bank of International Settlement?

☛ Great Bear of Wall Street?

These men were considered some of the world's most successful of their day.

Now, 80 years later, the history book asks us if we know what ultimately became of them.

The answers:

☛ The president of the largest steel company, Charles Schwab, died a pauper.

☛ The president of the largest gas company, Edward Hopson, went insane.

☛ The president of the NYSE, Richard Whitney, was released from prison to die at home.

☛ The greatest wheat speculator, Arthur Cooger, died abroad, penniless.

☛ The president of the Bank of International Settlement shot himself.

☛ The Great Bear of Wall Street, Cosabee Livermore, also committed suicide.

MORE FUN WITH HOCKEY   213

However, in that same year, 1923, Clint Benedict won the Stanley Cup with the Ottawa Senators. He played hockey until he was 80 and died in 1976 at the age of 84. He was financially secure at the time of his death.

The moral: Screw work. Play hockey.

Heaven or Hell

An ardent hockey player dies and finds himself at the Pearly Gates.

St. Peter tells the man he has lived an exemplary life and that he can go right in.

The man asks, "St. Peter, where is the hockey rink?"

"I'm terribly sorry," replies St. Peter, "but that's one thing we don't have here."

The man turns and decides to see if the situation is any better in hell. On the road to hell, he is greeted by the devil, who has already heard of the hockey player's rejection of heaven.

"This way, sir," says the devil. "Here is the finest professional rink you are likely to find this side of Canada."

The hockey player looks around and agrees that it is the finest arena he has ever seen. He decides he'd rather spend eternity there than in heaven, and he signs up for the full package.

"So," he says to the devil, "why don't you go get me some sticks and pucks and I'll have the game of my afterlife."

"I'm sorry, sir, we don't have any."

"What?" says the man. "No sticks or pucks for a fine rink like this?"

"No, sir," says the devil fiendishly. "That's the hell of it."

A Sin to Play on Sunday

After church one Sunday, one of the congregants walks up to the priest and says, "Father, is it a sin to play hockey on Sunday?

"My son," says the priest, putting his hand on the man's shoulder, "I've seen you play hockey. It's a sin any day."

Jesus and Sidney Crosby are playing golf. It's Crosby's turn to tee off, and he does so on a long par five. It's a great drive straight up the fairway, and he's about a seven iron off the green. "Not bad," Jesus says. Jesus then steps up to tee off, and he too hits a great shot, but it's not anywhere near as close as Crosby's first shot.

Just as the ball comes to a stop, a gopher pops out of its hole, grabs Jesus' ball in its mouth and runs up the fairway. Before it can get even 20 feet, an eagle swoops down out of the heavens, grabs the gopher in its mouth and flies off toward the green. Just as the ball, eagle and gopher get above the hole, a lightning bolt strikes out of a cloudless sky and vaporizes both the eagle and the gopher.

The ball drops straight down into the hole for a hole-in-one.

Jesus looks up and says, "Dad! Please! I'd rather do it myself!"

Rick Stevens: Avid Hockey Player and Male Rights Activist Final Notes

Open letter to all men:

It is important for men to remember that, as women grow older, it becomes harder for them to maintain the same quality of housekeeping as when they were younger. When you notice this, try not to yell at them. Some are oversensitive, and there's nothing worse than an oversensitive woman.

My name is Rick. Let me relate how I handled the situation with my wife, Rachel. When I retired a few years ago, it became necessary for Rachel to get a full-time job, along with her part-time job, both for extra income and for the health benefits that we needed. Shortly after she started working, I noticed she was beginning to show her age. I usually get home from hockey practice about the same time she gets home from work. Although she knows how hungry I am, she almost always says she has to rest for half an hour or so before she starts dinner. I don't yell at her. Instead, I tell her to take her time and just tell me when she gets dinner on the table. I generally have lunch at the Men's Grill near the arena, so eating out is not reasonable. I'm ready for some home-cooked grub when I hit the door.

She used to do the dishes as soon as we finished eating. But now it's not unusual for them to sit on the table for several hours after dinner. I do what I can by diplomatically reminding her several times each evening that they won't clean themselves. I know she really appreciates this, as it does seem to motivate her to get them done before she goes to bed.

Another symptom of aging is complaining, I think. For example, she will say that it is difficult for her to find time to pay the monthly bills during her lunch hour. But, boys, we take 'em for better or worse, so I just smile and offer encouragement. I tell her to stretch it out over two, or even three days. That way, she won't have to rush so much. I also remind her that missing lunch completely now and then wouldn't hurt her any (if you know what I mean). I like to think tact is one of my strong points.

When doing simple jobs, she seems to think she needs more rest periods. She had to take a break when she was only half-finished mowing the yard. I try not to make a scene. I'm a fair man. I tell her to fix herself a nice, big, cold glass of freshly squeezed lemonade and just sit for a while. And, as long as she is making one for herself, she may as well make one for me, too.

I know that I probably look like a saint in the way I support Rachel. I'm not saying that showing this much consideration is easy. Many men will find it difficult. Some will find it impossible! Nobody knows better than I do how frustrating women get as they get older. However, guys, even if you just use a little more tact and less criticism of your aging wife because of this article, I will consider that writing it was well worthwhile. After all, we are put on this earth to help each other.

Signed,

Rick Stevens

EDITOR'S NOTE: Rick died suddenly on January 31 of a perforated rectum. The police report says he was found with a Sherwood graphite extra long stick jammed up his rear end, with just the blade showing, and a sledgehammer lying nearby. His wife, Rachel, was arrested and charged with murder. The all-woman jury took only 10 minutes to find her Not Guilty, accepting her defense that Rick, somehow without looking, accidentally sat down on his hockey stick.

Why Single Guys Are Skinny

I attended a hockey convention in Montreal over the winter and was somewhat interested in the result of one particular study performed on hockey players; specifically I was interested in evening league players. This study indicated that the single gentlemen who play in these leagues are skinnier than the married ones.

The reason for this phenomenon is actually quite simple. The single hockey player goes out and plays his game, has a refreshment after the game in the locker room, goes home and goes to his refrigerator. He finds nothing decent there, so he goes to bed.

The married hockey player goes out and plays his game, has a refreshment after the game in the locker room, goes home and goes to bed. He finds nothing decent there, so he goes to his refrigerator.

Pauses

A Saudi royal is attending his first hockey game at Air Canada Centre and starts complaining to his hosts about all the interruptions and intermissions.

"I presume such pauses are required to permit the players a rest," he says.

"No," comes the reply. "They permit the spectators to catch their breath."

The Toronto Maple Leafs are sponsoring a banquet for their hockey legends. The Bishop of Toronto sits at the head of the table and is called upon to say grace. He must be excited to rub shoulders with some of the greatest names in hockey because he is a little flustered.

"Thank you Lord, for what we are about to eat," he says, and then concludes, "In the name of the Father, the Son and the Goalie Host."

Tourist

While out sport fishing off the Florida coast, a Montreal Canadiens fan capsizes his boat. He can swim, but his fear of alligators keeps him clinging to the overturned craft.

Spotting a Tampa Bay Lightning fan standing on the shore, the tourist shouts: "Are there any gators around here?"

"Naw," the man hollers back. "They ain't been around for years!"

Feeling safe, the Canadiens fan starts swimming leisurely toward the shore. When he is about halfway there, he asks the guy, "How'd you get rid of the gators?"

"We didn't do nothin'," the Lightning fan replies. "The sharks got 'em."

When young Jose, newly arrived in the United States, makes his first trip to Madison Square Garden, there are no tickets left for sale. Touched by his disappointment, a friendly ticket salesman finds him a perch near the American flag in the rafters. Later, Jose writes home enthusiastically about his experience. "And the Americans, they are so friendly!" he concludes. "Before the game started, they all stood up and looked at me and sang...'Jose, can you see?'"

Great Day!

Father Francis Norton wakes up Sunday morning and, realizing it is an exceptionally beautiful sunny day, decides he just has to play a little hockey outside by himself. So he tells the associate pastor that he is feeling sick and convinces him to say Mass that day.

As soon as the associate pastor leaves the room, Father Norton heads out of town to a hockey rink about 40 miles away. This way he knows he won't accidentally meet anyone from his parish. Strapping on his skates, he has a clean sheet of ice for himself. After all, it is Sunday morning and everyone else is in church.

At about this time, Saint Peter leans over to the Lord while looking down from the heavens and exclaims, "You're not going to let him get away with this, are you?"

The Lord sighs, "No, I guess not."

Just then the Pittsburgh Penguins team bus shows up, and Father Norton gets to play on the same line as Sidney Crosby for the rest of the morning. St. Peter is astonished. He looks at the Lord and asks, "Why did you let him do that?"

The Lord smiles and replies, "Who's he going to tell?"

Hockey Giver

Zach Parise is out driving in his Rolls Royce when he spots two men on the roadside eating handfuls of grass. Parise stops and asks them why they are eating grass.

"We don't have any money for food. Grass is all we can get," says one of the men.

MORE FUN WITH HOCKEY   221

"Then come with me," says Parise. "I'll help you out."

"But I have a wife and two children," says the man.

"Bring them, too. And bring your friend there," says Parise.

The second man replies, "Thank you, sir, but I have a wife and six children."

"Bring them, too," says Parise. "You're all coming to my mansion. The more the merrier."

"God bless you for your kind heart, sir," says the first man.

"It's no trouble at all," says Parise. "My mower is broken, and the grass in my garden must be 3 feet high."

Accidental

A hockey player is involved in a terrible car crash and is rushed to the hospital. Just before he is put under, the surgeon pops in to see him. "I have some good news and some bad news," says the surgeon. "The bad news is that I have to remove your right arm."

"Oh, no!" cries the man. "My hockey career is over! Please, doc, what's the good news?"

"The good news is, I have another one to replace it with, but it's a woman's arm. I'll need your permission before I go ahead with the transplant"

"Go for it, doc," says the man. "As long as I can play hockey again."

The operation goes well, and a year later the man is out on the ice when he bumps into the surgeon. "Hi, how's the new arm?" asks the surgeon.

"Just great," says the hockey player. "I'm playing the best hockey of my life. My new arm has a much finer touch and my wrist shot has really improved."

"That's great," says the surgeon.

"Not only that," continues the hockey player, "my handwriting has improved, I've learned how to sew my own clothes and I've even taken up painting landscapes in water colors."

"Unbelievable!" says the surgeon. "I'm so glad to hear the transplant was such a great success. I'm glad you didn't have any negative side effects."

"Well, there's just one problem," says the hockey player. "Every time I get an erection, I also get a headache!"

Poor Wifey

A woman is having an affair with the TV repairman. She complains to him, "My husband never pays any attention to me—all he's ever bothered about is watching the latest hockey game on TV. That's why we've got the biggest HDTV in the city—so he can watch all the games."

Suddenly she hears the key in the front door. Her husband has unexpectedly arrived home early from work. She says to her lover, "Quick, hide behind the TV."

MORE FUN WITH HOCKEY   223

So the lover hides behind the TV, while the husband gets a beer and sits down to watch the hockey game. After a half an hour, the lover is getting really uncomfortable behind the television. Eventually he simply walks out, going straight past the husband and out the front door.

The husband turns to his wife and says, "Hey, honey, I didn't see the referee send that guy off, did you?"

Balls

Every year Jim's father asks him what he wants for his birthday, and every year Jim says he wants a pink hockey puck. For years and years it is the only gift he ever requests. While other kids want the latest toys or new electronics, Jim only wants a pink hockey puck. On his birthday, he wants a pink hockey puck; for Christmas, he wants more pink pucks. His father tries to tempt him with the latest "in" thing, but nothing else interests him.

Eventually, Jim's dad gets tired of buying his son pink pucks, so for his 18th birthday, he gets Jim a surprise—a brand new sports car. Jim likes the car and takes it into town for a spin. Passing a sports store, he sees that they have some pink hockey pucks in the window, so he parks on the side of the road and gets out to take a better look. Halfway across the road, he gets hit by a truck. Jim's father comes to see him in the hospital. He knows Jim isn't going to make it and wants to ask his son one question before he dies. "Jim," he says.

"You've never played hockey in your life, so why all these years did you want pink pucks as gifts?"

Jim looks up at his father, opens his mouth to speak and dies.

And the moral of the story is, you should always look both ways before crossing the street.

CHAPTER 10

Diary of a Locked-out NHLer

Day 1
OMG! Just found out that my BFFs are going on strike. I am getting, like, a million texts right now.

Day 2
Okay, so I think this thing will be resolved soon. I mean we are fighting over millions of dollars one way or the other. Things aren't that bad for us.

Day 3
Since nothing is happening I'm going to hit the tanning salon. All that time in the gym and on the ice has left me a little pasty. I was going to call Sean Avery, but he is probably there already.

Day 4
Spent the day tweeting cool Instagram pictures of my bulldog. Got a thousand likes!

Day 5
Woke up in a daze. Went down to the rink with all my equipment, then I got dressed and hit the ice only to interrupt a girls ringette game. They wouldn't let me play. After getting home, sat on the couch and turned on TSN only to hear reports on some sports called b.a.s.k.e.t.b.a.l.l and s.o.c.c.e.r. Needed a hockey fix bad, so I watched *Mighty Ducks* twice.

Day 6

Woke up. Went down to the gym just to shower. Miss the guys! Called my agent and suggested he maybe get me an acting gig if this lockout goes on much longer.

Still up at 1:00 AM, decided to make a crank call to Gary Bettman. Called him a midget Napolean wannabee with no soul.

Day 15

Called up a few of the guys to see what they were doing. Talked about hockey for a bit but ended up sharing our favorite turkey recipes as Thanksgiving approaches.

Day 25

Decided to grow a lockout beard. It's been a few days now. I think I will keep it.

Day 30

Girlfriend made me shave my beard. Now she has me looking at schools to refocus my career in case the lockout never ends. I was thinking of becoming a welder or maybe taking over my mom's B&B in Collingwood. Or maybe a dietician. I hope hockey comes back.

Day 32

Taking a day off from working out. I am getting tired and bored of this lockout. I rented a bunch of movies, got a bunch of junk food and beer and had a "me" day. It was nice.

Day 45

Went to visit my parents. Got to sit in my old basement and look through my old collection of hockey cards. Man those guys in the 1980s had it good. All hair, beer and cigarettes between periods, and no worries. Now I have lockouts, CBA negotiations every year it seems, and fans that hate me. Mom is making cookies upstairs. Yeah, home!

Day 50

Okay, this is nuts. We are not asking for much. We just want what is ours and what is owed to us. Is that such a bad thing? We keep getting screwed over by Bettman and his cohorts, and we can't take it anymore. Soon the NHL will be busting into my house and taking the equipment they gave me. I even heard a story that the Canadiens asked Cammelleri to pay for a jersey he took after they traded him. We players must rise up against our oppressors and start a revolution. For too long my people have suffered. They have taken our hockey away from us too many times. And while they live high off the hog, smoking their cigars and drinking their cognac with Puff Daddy from golden goblets, we sit in our BMWs wondering if we will ever be able to afford a Mercedes or Porsche, like the one I've had my eye on. RISE UP. These industrial pigs cannot take advantage of us anymore. Fellow hockey lovers UNITE and march with me in full gear on New

> The three important elements of hockey are forecheck, backcheck and paycheck.
>
> –Gil Perreault

York and have our voices heard! I am calling for a million hockey players to march on the NHL headquarters. I call for peace, but bring your sticks and strap your skates to your hands, for we will bathe the streets in blood before we are silenced. FREE HOCKEY! FREE HOCKEY! FREE HOCKEY! *SIC SEMPER TYRANNIS!*

Day 55

All work and no play make Jack a dull boy.

All work and no play make Jack a dull boy.

All work and no play make Jack a dull boy.

All work and no play make Jack a dull boy.

All work and no play make Jack a dull boy.

All work and no play make Jack a dull boy.

All work and no play make Jack a dull boy.

All work and no play make Jack a dull boy.

Day 60

Gary Bettman. GARY BETTMAN. BettMAN! B...E...T...T..M...A...N!!!!!! GARYYYYYY GARYYYYYYY! BETTMAN!!!!!!! I see you Gary Bettman. Are you a betting man, Gary? Would you like to play a game with me Mr. Gary? Mister NHL Boss. I would like to play a game. Would you like to play a little game? Muahahahahaha!

Day 65

Visiting a (cough) doctor today to talk about things. Not well. Not well at all.

Day 85

Well, after a little time to myself, I am taking the doctor's orders and getting back on the ice. I have organized a few local games in the area and will be teaching a few kids a thing or two about hockey. Start small, and we will see where this goes. The doctor says getting out and meeting people will make me feel better.

Day 90

That's it, I'm going to Vegas! Taking my man Evander Kane with me. It's hard not having any work. This lockout has really affected the players' salaries.

Day 91

Won mad money, yo! Took a photo of my boy Kane with some of his winnings. Told him not to Tweet it, given that some of the fans might not look upon a player holding stacks of cash as a good thing during the lockout. I don't think he listened.

Day 99

Man they should totally get a hockey team here. Screw Winterpeg! I wanna play out of Vegas, baby! Casinos and showgirls after hockey games. Yeah! And maybe a Celine concert. But don't tell anyone.

Day 100

Ok, I broke down and went to see Celine. It was magical!

Day 101

Back from Vegas. Ugh!

Day 105

There are rumors buzzing around that the lockout might end. Got a bunch of Tweets and texts from buddies saying things are looking good. Started airing out my gear in prep.

Day 106

Someone called Gary Bettman a troll, and now the talks are off. Damn! I thought we had it.

Day 107

Okay, Donald Fehr has apologized to Gary and made Shane Doan promise never to call him names 'cause it hurts his feelings. Talks are back on!

Day 119

HOORAY! It's finally over! I get to see my buddies and play hockey again! Yes! I am so happy I'm jumping for joy!

Day 120

Got too excited jumping on the bed, fell off, knocked my head, and now I'm out 3 to 4 weeks with a concussion!

Notes on Sources

Web Sources

http://sports.nationalpost.com/2012/09/19/stanley-cup-will-stay-put-even-if-nhl-season-is-cancelled/

http://blogs.thescore.com/nhl/2012/10/31/johnny-oduya-has-chosen-the-unconventional-nhl-lockout-route-thailand/

http://www.facebook.com/pages/Just-Drop-It/480181678699361

http://sports.yahoo.com/blogs/nhl-puck-daddy/stanley-cup-terrible-idead-winnipeg-media-vs-evander-160453833--nhl.html#more-46776

http://ca.sports.yahoo.com/blogs/nhl-puck-daddy/tyler-bozak-joins-nhl-halloween-blackface-club-michael-041546005--nhl.html

http://sports.yahoo.com/blogs/nhl-puck-daddy/girl-isn-t-shaving-her-legs-until-nhl-163955784--nhl.html

http://sports.yahoo.com/blogs/nhl-puck-daddy/no-winter-classic-harlem-globetrotters-announce-out-door-ice-210246444--nhl.html

http://sports.yahoo.com/blogs/nhl-puck-daddy/revisit-2012-nhl-lockout-miserable-glory-video-144335814--nhl.html

http://ca.sports.yahoo.com/blogs/nhl-puck-daddy/nhl-fan-boycott-support-just-drop-initiative-eye-220337071--nhl.html

http://www.cbc.ca/player/Sports/Hockey/ID/2323644508/

J. Alexander Poulton is a writer, photographer and genuine enthusiast of Canada's national pastime. A resident of Montreal all his life, he has developed a healthy passion for hockey ever since he saw his first Montreal Canadiens game. His favorite memory was meeting the legendary gentleman hockey player Jean Beliveau, who in 1988 towered over the young awe-struck author.

He earned his B.A in English Literature from McGill University and his graduate diploma in Journalism from Concordia University. He has more than 25 sports books to his credit, including *Canadian Hockey Record Breakers, Greatest Moments in Canadian Hockey, Greatest Games of the Stanley Cup, Canadian Hockey Trivia, Hockey's Hottest Defensemen, The Montréal Canadiens, The Toronto Maple Leafs, Sidney Crosby, Does This Make Me Look Fat? Canadian Sport Humour* and *A History of Hockey in Canada*.